A Patriot After All

A Patriot After All

The Story of a Chicano Vietnam Vet

JUAN RAMIREZ

University of New Mexico Press
Albuquerque

The following authors generously have granted permission to reprint their poems: Jan
Barry for "The Longest War" and Frank A. Cross, Jr., for "Thoughts of an Infantryman
Observing the Body of an NVA Soldier," both poems originally published in *Winning
Hearts and Minds: War Poems by Vietnam Veterans,* edited by Larry Rottman, Jan Barry,
and Basil T. Paquet, copyright 1972 by 1st Casualty Press; W. D. Erhart for "The One
That Died," originally published in *To Those Who Have Gone Home Tired: New &
Selected Poems,* Thunder's Mouth Press, New York, 1984; Renny Christopher for "Viet
Nam And California," "Combat," "Viet Nam and El Salvador, and on and on
forever . . . ," and " 'There is no boot camp for Viet Nam vets' wives'," from *Viet Nam
and California,* Vietnam Generation Inc. and Burning Cities Press, 1998.

Some names have been changed to protect the identities of some people in this book.

Library of Congress Cataloging-in-Publication Data
Ramirez, Juan, 1949–
A patriot after all : the story of a Chicano Vietnam vet / Juan
Ramirez. — 1st ed.
p.   cm.
ISBN 0-8263-1958-0 (cloth). — ISBN 0-8263-1959-9 (pbk.)
1. Vietnamese Conflict, 1961–1975 — Participation, Mexican
American.   2. Vietnamese Conflict, 1961–1975 — Personal narratives,
American.   3. Ramirez, Juan, 1949–   .   4. Mexican American
families — United States.   5. Mexican American soldiers — Vietnam.
I. Title.
DS559.8.M39R36   1999
959.704'3372 — dc21   98-46679
                                                                    CIP

Contents

Acknowledgments

When I first wrote this book in 1986, I did not do it intending to write a book. It started out as an undergraduate senior thesis with my personal experiences in Vietnam as its core and took approximately six months of full-time work to finish.

The opportunity to turn my thesis into a published book came through a graduate student at the University of California at Santa Cruz named Renny Christopher, back in 1992, when she asked to use a small excerpt from my manuscript in her dissertation. She has since received her doctorate in American literature and has had her dissertation published by the University of Massachusetts Press, and she has published a book of poetry as well.

Without Renny's interest in and use of my work, I would not have been motivated to return to the manuscript for revisions and additions to make it into the book it now is. I must also say that if I had not had Renny's support, encouragement, and mentorship over the last two years, I could not have finished it. She gave me countless hours of her scarce time. She gave me and my work the kind of devotion that she gives every day in her classrooms. She is the kind of teacher that all students should get to experience at least once in their school careers. She is the best example of what a teacher should be. To have had her help with the final editing was in itself a gift of time and energy I will forever cherish because I was totally lost as to how and where to start. Thank you, Renny you're a very special human being.

I am also very grateful to all my family who helped with their time, support, and love, in particular my wife, Linda, and my sister-in-law, Cathy, who both typed and typed, enduring my awful longhand for the last two years. A very special thank-you to my youngest brother, Paco, who has loved me and been my biggest fan in life no matter what I've done.

I want also to thank all my friends who have helped me with my readjustment journey through the years, like David Heaston, Mark Sandman, Joanna Kranich, Joe Splane, Michele Shippen, Bob Shippen, Dan Scripture, Bob Gallagher, Joe Fernandez, Barry Jones, Woody Bookout, and many, many others who still cared.

But most of all I want to thank my wife, Linda, who has put up with many of my ups and downs through this work and our lives together for the last twenty years.

Finally, a word about my father. My father passed away in the summer of 1997 and will never read this story, but I know he would be proud. Although his life as I have told it may seem sad and bleak, he did in the end arrive at some peace with himself. He was a hero to all of us, friends and family, as well as a patriot to this country. He had his problems, but he was a good man, a loving man. He died with dignity, the same kind of dignity he carried and lived throughout his life. Thank you, Pop, for my life and who I am and all that you sacrificed for us.

A Dedication

To all of you who have died
and have been long since
forgotten by most of us,
I promise your spirits that
I will work to make your
sacrifice honorable and
meaningful by fighting to
contribute to the end of war.
Because if we continue to be
warlike, then indeed the
sacrifices of you who died
in the name of humanity and
the end of all wars will have
been for nothing.

The Longest War

The longest war is over
Or so they say
Again
But I can still hear the gunfire
Every night
From
My bed.
The longest nightmare
Never seems to
Ever
Quite come
To
An end.

Jan Barry

Viet Nam and California

On my map
the two coastlines —
California's
Viet Nam's —
look like they should fit
as jigsaw pieces
if only I could bring them together
at just the right angle.

In the Sacramento River delta
in the center of a park
near the capitol building
a memorial lists the names
of all the California boys
who died in the war.
From the desert to the forest to the beach,
Inyo, Guerneville, Twain Harte, Santa Cruz,
Vacaville, Los Angeles, Bakersfield, San Martin:
six boys from my hometown.

In the delta of the Mekong River
or the Black River,
in Saigon, Hanoi,
An Loc, Qui Nhon, Di An, Chu Lai,
in every town
a monument rises above the roofs
of thatch or tile.
Inscribed
Tó Quóc Ghi Cúng Cáe Liêt Sĩ —
"The fatherland remembers the sacrifice
of the fallen heroes."

These stones
memorialize the boys
killed by the boys
from my hometown.

Renny Christopher

Part One

BEFORE

One

FAMILY

I was born in Palo Alto, California, in 1949, part of the baby boom generation in statistical fact if not in cultural fact. My parents were first- and second-generation Americans of Mexican descent who now refer to themselves as Chicanos. My mother, the oldest of seven children, was born in Santa Clara, California. My father, the oldest of the seven Ramirez children, was born in his mother's house in Redwood City, California. I have always thought of myself as a Californian, although what I mean by that has shifted over the years as I went through different phases of my life — a kid whose main interest was baseball, a marine in Vietnam, a late entry college student trying to get involved with the Chicano civil rights movement, and then, later, a small-business owner just trying to live a life.

As part of trying to understand my own life, I've tried to understand the history of my family as immigrants and as Americans. On my mother's side of the family, my great-grandparents are the immigrant generation. My maternal great-grandmother, Angelita Cortez Bautista, was born in Toyahua, Zacatecas, Mexico, and came to California at the age of fourteen. Until the day she died, she regretted leaving Mexico. Angelita was, according to my mother, a very angry woman who sometimes drank to excess. When she would get drunk, she would sometimes pull out her gun and fire shots into the walls and ceiling, crying and sobbing about her beloved Mexico. Sometimes she would celebrate in the same way, giving out *gritos,* or loud cries, long into the night, "just like they used to at home."

Maybe Angelita was an angry woman because she was so sad and wounded. She never loved her first husband, my great-grandfather, Pedro Bautista. She had been chosen by him, and a marriage was arranged in the traditional fashion. Pedro Bautista's ambition made him want to take his new wife to the United States for a better life. The couple came north in about 1910. Angelita used to brag that she came to the United States "the civilized way," by train as a paid passenger wearing fine clothes. She said she wore long white beautiful gloves with shoes and a hat to match.

They settled in La Puente, California, and had six children, five girls and one boy. Antonia, my grandmother, was the first, born in 1912, then came Ruth and her twin — the twin died at the age of thirteen of a mysterious illness — then Evelyn, Frances, and Frank. Pedro's position as a ranch foreman paid good money, and they were able to build their own house. Life was good enough for them for twelve years; then it all changed when Pedro was killed in a farming accident.

After Pedro's death, my great-grandmother and her children left La Puente with Rafael Chavez, the man who was my great-grandmother's lover even while she had been married to Pedro. My great-grandmother and her children started working the various fields of central California, picking apricots, cotton, and peaches but mostly grapes. Rafael had been working the fields already, so he knew the circuit. Eventually Angelita and Rafael got married, and she was much happier in marriage with Rafael, but they had little else to their name.

The transient life of field work was and still is very hard. Whenever my great-aunts talk about those times, it is with little nostalgia and much bitterness. Unlike my mother, they do not have romantic memories of those days. In fact, two of my great-aunts, Evelyn and Frances, and my grandmother, Antonia, refuse to discuss this part of their lives at all, saying only, "Why talk about it now? Those were not good times. Those days are best forgotten, not remembered." But my great-aunt Ruth, or Cuca, talks about those days easily and frankly.

Cuca, although very respectful of her mother, resents her for making all of her siblings work so hard as children. Actually all the Bautista women talk about their mother with a combination of fear, resentment, and respect but with little fondness or love. As a child I knew Angelita as my grandmother and thought of her in this way for many years, even after I was told the truth. I best remember her as someone who was, at least in her later years, very overweight, huge to us. Her size was like her presence in the family, much like a huge dark cloud of fear. I did feel love from her, but it was scarce and hard to hold on to.

Angelita's daughter, my grandmother, Antonia, had many different "boyfriends." In fact, her first three children — Aurora, my mother; Tony; and Gloria — were from different men. My mother never knew her father. He had left before she was born.

My mother grew up believing that Rafael Chavez was her father and Angelita her mother. She became angry when she found out that Antonia was her mother. She blamed not Angelita but Antonia. She harbored resentment for Antonia for most of her adult life, to the point that she forbade my sisters, brothers, and me to recognize Antonia as our grandmother. We were to call her by her name only, Antonia.

I have had a much closer, warmer, and more intimate relationship with my father's side of the family, although they're no less troubled. They are perhaps even more tragic than my mother's side of the family because the alcoholism on my father's side was much more deadly.

My paternal grandmother came to the United States by way of freight car through Nogales, Arizona, with her two oldest sons, Peter and Jesse. I know very little about the ex-husband she was leaving behind in Mexico, only that he was cruel and abusive. She came to the United States looking for a better life and to escape poverty. Whenever I hear or tell the story of her journey, I have such strong feelings about it, I can almost see and touch her. I can feel the discomfort of the freight car. Cold and damp and dark, filled with barnyard odors. Children crying, and old people coughing and wheezing. I feel angry and sad when I think of it, just like the first time I heard the story. I could barely stand the image of my "Mama" suffering in any kind of way. At the same time, this mental image shows me a heroine, a woman of strength and courage. I can see her lean and beautiful face smiling through all of it.

My grandmother met Refufio Ramirez while traveling to the United States. They ended up in Redwood City, California, in about 1925. Mama had five sons and two daughters with Refufio Ramirez. My father, John, was born at his mother's house in a neighborhood called Five Points, an area that is known now as Woodside Road and Main, just west of El Camino Real in Redwood City. The family lived in two different houses in Redwood City, the Five Points house and then the Spruce Street house. I grew to love and remember always the Spruce Street house. Our family started out there, living in a garage turned into an apartment.

My grandmother Ramirez, Mama as I called her, was perhaps the most significant person in my life. She was tall for a Mexican woman, maybe five-foot six or seven, and slender and lean. Behind her glasses was a distinctive Indian face, kind of gaunt with high cheekbones. Her complexion was very brown. She kept her hair in a bun most of the time, but it was long and black. My dad and all the other Ramirez children have her body type, complexion, and facial features, as do most of my siblings and I. Her most prominent feature was her hands. I used to hold them with great fondness. Putting them against my face would make me feel warm and safe. They were strong, weathered hands; beautiful and graceful as well. I was fascinated with her long lean fingers because they were just like my dad's.

Her house and garden hold memories I will cherish forever. Living there was like a holiday every day. It was an enormous old house, not quite your typical Victorian, that sat high off ground level with cement steps about ten feet wide and six to eight feet high. My cousins and I used to play and hang out on those steps. My dad said my grandmother bought and paid for the Spruce Street house herself with a little help from him and his brother Andy. She worked at a cannery for many years. Refufio, her husband, was a cruel and selfish man who worked but kept his money for his liquor and gambling. At some point he left. My grandmother also sold rabbits and chickens she raised. She sold her own fruit and vegetables as well. Playing in her garden was not allowed, but I could help work in it if I didn't hurt anything. We lived with my grandmother until I was about four years old.

While we lived on Spruce Street, my mother often competed with my grandmother for my affections. My grandmother and I used to do many things together. We rode the train from Redwood City to San Jose, mostly to the only theater around that showed Mexican movies. We used to window-shop, too. I remember shoplifting little toys and my grandmother looking the other way, pretending not to notice. My mother tells that once, when my parents were arguing, my grandmother attempted to sneak me out through a window of our garage apartment. She took me from their house to hers, telling my mother that she was "still very young and could have more babies, so why not leave him with me and you live here." But my mother called the police, and they made her give me back.

I am glad I grew up around my grandmother Ramirez. So many images of those times dwell in my consciousness, like lifesavers helping me through an ocean of turmoil and sadness. It is only now that I fully appreciate her importance. No one else loved me and made me feel as special as she.

There was another side to Mama that was difficult to understand, a paradox if you will. She loved birds very much. On her back porch she had many cages and feeders for her domestic and wild birds. Sometimes cats would manage to kill even the birds in cages. Once when I was six or seven years old, she made it a point to give me a lesson on cats. First she told me that cats were evil animals possessed by evil human spirits. Since they were of no value, she felt it best to eliminate as many cats as possible. She used different methods — poison, drowning — but one method in particular was very disturbing to me. She would trap or capture two, three, or four cats, keeping them alive until she had enough. Then she would put them all into a burlap gunnysack, tie a rope around the opening, and throw one end of the rope up and around a cross member of the grape arbor, hanging the sack full of cats from the arbor. She would then tie off the other end of the rope so the sack could swing like a piñata. At first I thought this was going to be fun — maybe we were just going to scare them. But it was to be much more awful than I imagined. After the sack stopped swinging, she grabbed a baseball bat that was leaning against a post and, with a most devilish grin, started hitting the sack filled with cats, hitting it harder each time. The cats were screaming and howling like I had never heard before or since. She kept hitting them and hitting them. Soon the sack was soaked through and dripping with blood. Mama was worked into a frenzy. I was scared. I had never seen her like this. She stopped long enough to offer me the bat so I could hit the cats, but I couldn't do it. The only word to describe her reaction is shame. This side of her manifested itself in another way, too. Toward my cousin Ivy.

Ivy, who is about two years younger than me, is the oldest of my aunt Teresa's eight children. Ivy and her mother and siblings always lived with my grandmother Ramirez — while we did and after. It's a long story, but I believe my grandmother hated Ivy's father so much that she took it out on Ivy. It is hard for me to visualize my Mama's house without Ivy's sad little face looking out a window. She was always in the house watching us play, either because she was being punished or doing chores. Mama's house was a prison for her. Mama beat Ivy more frequently and more fiercely than any of the other kids. Even though Ivy and I are both recovering now from alcohol and drug abuse, she has had far more difficulties in her life than I have. She was in and out of jail and programs and halfway houses and was homeless at times. Her mother, my aunt Teresa, died from alcoholism at age thirty-nine when Ivy was only twenty. My cousin was lost and lonely for many years. The relationship I had with Mama was quite different from Ivy's. I am eternally grateful yet somewhat guilt ridden about this contrast. It is only now, some thirty years after Grandma Ramirez's death, that I am able to accept both realities. Mama made me feel like I was special and worthwhile. She took time with me, explained things to me, turned life's daily demands into lessons for me. It is sad that Mama didn't treat all her grandchildren the same way, because her influence has been critical to my survival.

My parents were young and ignorant when they met. My mother was sixteen and my father was twenty when they were introduced at my paternal great-grandmother's funeral. My parents had experienced harsh and difficult young lives, and they were determined to make things better for themselves and for their future children. Living with her grandmother was becoming more and more oppressive to my mother. She saw marriage as a way out and took it.

My mother, Aurora, was an attractive young lady, which was a curse in her family. They thought because she was the daughter of a woman who was also very attractive and, in their opinion, loose and easy, my mother would turn out the same. She was constantly watched by her great-grandmother and by her aunts, especially where boys were involved. Mom is light complected, much like her grandmother but different than her mother, Antonia, who is dark and has strong Indian features. Mom's hair was black, creating a striking contrast with her fair skin. She liked it that people sometimes told her she looked like Elizabeth Taylor.

My dad was tall among Mexicans, as were his brothers. He was, and I note this in the past tense because he seems to have shrunk, about five-foot eleven. He was and still is a handsome man. His complexion is dark brown and his eyes are dark brown, almost black. His hair is, even in his late sixties, full and black. Of course, now he has a lot of gray as well. His face resembles his mother's, lean and gaunt. He has large full lips and very high cheekbones, with a somewhat large nose. I used to tell him he looked like Nat King Cole, meaning it as a compliment. But he didn't like it, although he did like Nat's music.

Being the oldest Ramirez boy, my father assumed fatherly roles early. Although my dad and his siblings had some high school education, none of them ever actually graduated. The same thing is true for my mother and her sister Gloria. My mother never attended school past the eighth grade. But my mother's brother Tony did graduate from high school and, in fact, was the first of his generation and the previous generation to do so. I would become the next to graduate from high school.

My father enlisted in the navy at the age of seventeen by lying about his age. It was 1944. Dad's two older brothers, Jesse and Peter, were already in the army, fighting Germans. Dad was on a landing support transport (LST), one of those ships that opens at the bow like a giant whale's mouth to let trucks, tanks, and men file onto the beach.

Dad doesn't talk much about anything deep, but I grew up hearing a lot about his war years. Although Dad's World War II and navy stories are mixed with resentment and pain, he is very proud of his service. I believe those times were a rite of passage for him; they also marked the end of a delusion he harbored about American society. Somehow he felt that if he did his part in this war, alongside all the other Americans, then somehow he and his kind would finally be accepted in their own country. As he puts it, "There were not many of us darkies in the navy." He grew up knowing that he was different and, for the most part, that he would not be accepted into mainstream society. To some extent he accepted this fact. After all, "We even spoke a different language," he would say, as if this were wrong. Not even in the midst of war could one expect some kind of honor among comrades-in-arms.

If not for his young age, Dad would have been treated even worse than he was. Many of his fellow sailors tried to protect him, primarily because they felt he was too young to be there. Many sailors hated him just because he was not white, but others looked after him as if he were their son. He made friends with some marines who were "darkies" like him. One in particular was a Puerto Rican from New York also named John. Dad admired John because he had already survived several island invasions. Their friendship ended when John did not return from an assignment. John had been killed assaulting a Japanese machine gun nest with his flamethrower. When he tells this story, Dad does not offer more details than that, obviously because it's too emotional. He cannot express the deep sense of loss over his friend's death. When I was born, he decided to call me John, Jr. — after his friend from the marines as much as after himself.

When he came home, much had changed. Job prospects were better and pay was better, but only for whites. The jobs available to my father were the same kind he had had before, although they were more plentiful and lucrative: field work, the tannery, the cement plant, and the cannery. He was surprised that his return as a war veteran did not bring him greater rewards. He thought people would treat him differently because he had that DD-214 paper, an honorable discharge. Many things had changed, but some things never do.

When he first returned from the war, he decided to try some field work. He hated it. He had never worked so hard for so little money, and he disliked the transient lifestyle altogether. After returning to Redwood City, he went back to working in the cannery and tannery.

If I pressed my dad for more of how he felt about the discrimination he experienced, he was always careful not to sound like he was complaining or whining. To my dad, racial prejudice is a fact of life. He resents it and, in his own way, struggles against it. His true hurt and outrage are quieted by a deep-seated conviction passed down to him by his mother that whatever obstacles Chicanos face in this country, they at least have a fighting chance to overcome them. Work hard and believe in God, and the rest would be taken care of. My father and his mother preached this lesson as if our lives depended on it. My father was always dreaming of that big chance when some boss would recognize his value and trust him with the kind of respect he deserved.

My parents developed personalities together that I view as complex dualities and contradictions — attitudes and values patched together like some kind of cross-cultural quilt, sometimes looking very interesting, other times looking very chaotic and wild, and sometimes seeming to make no sense at all. For a while it worked. My parents were determined to create a family unit, something that had been missing in their lives as children. They thought that achieving the American dream was the answer to all their pain. They also thought they could do this without compromising their Mexican cultural identity. They were both torn about who they were.

Mom is much more intensely proud of being Mexican, as this is what she was brought up to think. Her grandmother was always going on, especially when she was drunk, about how much she loved and missed Mexico. She would go on and on about how Americans had no manners, were loud, too aggressive, and pushy. Grandma Ramirez, on the other hand, did not like looking back to her life in Mexico. Like Grandma Bautista Cortez, she refused to learn English, and she often said in Spanish, "*¿Por qué hablar de ese país? No estaba nada bueno. No teníamos propiedad, no teníamos dinero, teníamos hambre todo el tiempo. ¿Que clase de vida es esa? No me voy a ir allí otra vez.*" "Why talk about that place? There was nothing good about it. We had no property, no money, and we were hungry all the time. What kind of life is that? I will never go back there." And she never did.

My father felt pride and shame for what he was. He resented the fact that he was treated differently, and he often confused being Mexican with not being good enough. He used this barrier to drive and motivate himself to be accepted as an equal. I think my father hated who he was because he thought he was a "sellout" who aspired to be and to have what the whites had. My mother is much the same except she takes the issue of race one step further and twists it with the belief that Mexican people and "our ways" are superior. Ironically, she also would say that she didn't want us "hanging around with that Mexican kid" or "I don't want you dressing like a Mexican," and above all, "I don't want you to sound like a Mexican."

My parents are fluent Spanish speakers, but they would not speak Spanish with their children. My mother denied us the opportunity and privilege of having two languages. She deliberately and systematically attempted to erase the Spanish language from our consciousnesses. Because my sister Evelyn and I were frequently at Grandma Ramirez's house, we had to speak Spanish to communicate with her. We also could only speak Spanish with Grandma Bautista, but we were not allowed to use it in any other situation and especially not at school, but that was not allowed, anyway.

The first house my parents purchased was a brand-new two-bedroom tract home in East Menlo Park. After a series of hard-labor jobs and working two and three jobs simultaneously, my dad found a good job at a new manufacturing plant in Palo Alto, making telephone and electrical power line products. He was happy and optimistic. My mother had jobs outside the home as well. Mom and Dad both worked hard to save enough money for the down payment and used dad's GI Bill benefits to buy the house. But what I remember most about living there was my dad's frightening alcoholic behavior, my own trouble in school, and noticing white people's fear of black people for the first time in my life.

I was about four years old when we moved to East Menlo Park. Although at the time my dad never missed work because of drinking, he would routinely get drunk on Friday night. He would get so drunk, he would barely make it home. Many times he would pass out in his car right in front of the house. Once he even slept in his car parked on the lawn all night.

We would be relieved if he passed out because he would terrorize us if he was conscious. Actually the worst was when he would have alcoholic blackouts. He would carry on for hours, talking, yelling, and hitting, and not remembering any of it the next day. Once he came home pounding on the door in a rage, yelling that my mother had some man inside because he could not open the door. He couldn't open the door because his key had broken off in the lock. We were all too scared to open the door. For a while, he quieted down. Suddenly his body came crashing in through a window headfirst. Just as suddenly — and frighteningly — he calmed down. It was as if he had witnessed his own madness and didn't like it. This was life with my father. He often would regret beating me and come to my room later, bringing me food or a toy, but he never really said he was sorry. I guess this is where I am supposed to say it wasn't that bad. I know he loved me. There were good times, too. But it was that bad.

My father worked hard and got his chance. He rose quickly in his job, getting better pay and more responsibility. As the promotions came, so did the new cars, television, hi-fi, bicycles, toys, and outings. His work became all consuming. Life was better in some ways but much more stressful in others. He would take it out on his children and his wife, and she would in turn take it out on us. My mother could become a frightening person herself. Not really having anything to compare it with then, I only now understand that the quality of their discipline could be called abusive.

I started school at Bell Haven Elementary in East Menlo Park. To say I had difficulty at school is putting it mildly. The first four years or so were dark, bleak, and lonely. I had to repeat the fourth grade. My only solace was visiting Grandma Ramirez as often as possible and playing with my sister Evelyn. "Evie" was a good sport. Traditionally she might be called a tomboy, a term I don't believe describes her accurately. She is two years younger than me, and she always struggled to keep up with me. Evie would try almost anything, no matter how difficult or dangerous. I would marvel at her tenacity and determination to hang with me. And it never felt like competition, more like bonding or camaraderie. She was indeed a buddy.

We lived in East Menlo Park approximately three years, and in that time our neighborhood became gripped with fear of the gradual integration of African-Americans. My father is somewhat of a bigot, which is still confusing to me. He discussed these attitudes with other adults, sending us kids away or whispering the way adults do when they are saying things too serious, scary, or foul for children's ears. My mother was not as worldly as my dad, and these racist attitudes seemed to both intrigue and perplex her. Years later she told me a story about when one of our neighbors came by to talk with her about "them." "They are taking over," this woman said to my mother. "They" were dirty and causing property values to decline. My mother says she was so naive that at first she thought the neighbor was talking about the infestation of dandelions in the lawn. When my mother realized the woman was talking about the black people moving into the neighborhood, she said she felt stupid.

There would be other such visits from our neighbors, spreading fear, bias, and intolerance like a virus. Out of ignorance and a need to feel like we belonged somewhere, we fell on the side of the whites. "Shush, maybe nobody has noticed we aren't white." We really weren't white, but given a choice, we certainly didn't want to be on the black side. We were struggling to be accepted, so if we were the lesser of these perceived evils, then so be it. As did many others, we moved away from East Menlo Park partly because of the influx of black families. We had other reasons for leaving, since our family was growing and we needed more room. My father's progress at work allowed us to move up in house size as well. We moved to Mountain View, approximately twenty miles south.

About that time, I finally found something that brought me a great deal of happiness: baseball. I had talent for it and, maybe more important, it became a vehicle by which to forge a special relationship with my father. It seemed to please him more that I was good at sports than the few subjects I did well in at school: geography, history, and writing. My father was not a good teacher, and doing homework together was normally a major ordeal. I can almost feel the heat of his anger and rage as he paced back and forth behind me because I was not getting whatever he was trying to explain. His anger was so powerful that he could paralyze me without hitting me. Sometimes even if I knew the answer, I was not able to form the words. But baseball was different. He was still impatient and hard on me when I was struggling, but he really seemed to enjoy playing ball with me, especially when I did well. Finally I had found something that got my father's attention without eliciting his anger. I became very good at other sports as well, but I *lived* baseball. I coveted my equipment and, like a favorite teddy bear, slept with my glove always. I even kept a ball in it, the newer the better. There was nothing like the smell of a new ball and glove, each similar but distinct in its own way. I often would go to sleep listening to a San Francisco Giants game on a small transistor radio.

Throughout my childhood and on into high school I was what a coach might call a steady, reliable player who gave his all every game. Like many boys, I carried the dream I would someday get a chance to play in the big leagues. I'm not sure when the dream started to fade, but I think my spirits took a mighty blow when my grandma Ramirez died. This is when other fantasies I held about life, God, and country started coming to an end.

My grandma Ramirez died in the summer of 1963, when I was in the seventh grade. She died suddenly in a sense but had been sick for a while, although no one knew how serious it was. She did not let on, refusing help or to go see a doctor. She believed they only made you worse. Sometimes I think she gave up trying because during the Christmas of 1961 her beloved home and garden burned to the ground. Christmas wrappings piled next to her woodstove somehow caught fire. No one was hurt except for her — her heart had been broken.

That house and garden were a part of her, and with them went her resolve.

She came to live with us in Mountain View but eventually found a place back in Redwood City. It was a much smaller house. I hated seeing my grandma living like that. She was so sad, and I could see the life slowly leaving her. She died in that house from pneumonia, a complication of the tuberculosis she had suffered years before. It made me angry at my mother. I blamed her and my father because I felt if she was with us, we could have taken care of her. I was devastated. I was angry at God, too. It just didn't seem fair.

When I went on to the eighth grade, I was put into a "special class," a remedial program separate from the mainstream or regular classes. As embarrassing as this was, I was somewhat numb to it all. I quit my religious training two weeks before my confirmation into the Catholic religion. Although my parents had compelled me to attend catechism twice a week, Saturday mornings and one weekday after school, they really did not "believe" themselves. But Grandma and I did. We used to have secret fun laughing at how truly soulless my parents were. It was as if we knew the truth about religious consciousness and they just faked it or, worse, did not have a clue. I also started drinking alcohol, something I used to promise my grandma I would never do. It made her so sad and angry when my dad and his brothers got drunk and fought with each other. I would tell her not to worry about me, that I would never drink and act like they did. She would just stare at me painfully and say, *"Ay, hijo, espero lo que no puede ser."* "Oh, son, I hope not."

My extended family also was coming apart at the seams. My dad became estranged from his brothers. He tried to take care of his sister and her kids, as he promised my grandmother, but it was more than he or anyone could do. Nobody seemed to notice. We were all too busy trying to find something to hang on to. My grandmother was the substance that held many lives together, and when she left, so did everything that was truly good, honest, and dignified about the family.

Grandma had been dead just over a year when I noticed television news reports about something happening in a distant country called Vietnam. It seems odd to me now that I would be concerned about the war at that point, but I vividly remember worrying that this so-called conflict would not be over by the time I graduated from high school in 1968. It scared me. Maybe somebody said something to me about it. Or maybe I just knew that this would be my rite of passage, too. After all, my father, uncles, and a few older cousins were in or had been in the military. I grew up listening to family stories about the military, men, and finally war. The stories always intrigued me, no matter how many times I heard them. Perhaps it was a given that I would serve also.

Watching the Vietnam War on television through those years was like watching a storm cloud working its way toward me. On the one hand, I welcomed it as part of the natural order of things. On the other hand, I worried because I just didn't know how bad it would be or how long it would last. I was scared a lot. I no longer had my grandma to help me. I was afraid of losing everything I had left, my family, my friends, and my own life. Although I never really discussed it, I worried that I would die in Vietnam, even long before I had made the decision to go there. But I had a twisted perception of how to deal with potential danger or conflict in those days. Instead of avoiding it like most sensible people, I would rush to it prematurely to get it over with. I played sports that way. I dealt with my parents that way. I fought other kids that way.

I entered Mountain View High School in 1964. I also started a new job the summer before school started. Other than sports, what I remember most vividly about high school is chasing after girls, hanging out with friends, and excessively drinking and brawling with whomever. I hung out with a mixed group of boys—Chicanos, Filipinos, Anglos, Portuguese, Spanish, Chinese, and Japanese kids. We were what they call jocks, and we were bullies. My family moved into another new house around that time, too.

After living on Spring Street for eight years, our family had grown to five children. Paco, the youngest, was about two years old when Grandma died. Dinora was two years older than Paco, and Joey, who was born deaf, was a year or so older than Dinora. Evie was the next oldest (and my chief rival for my father's attention). My dad was still making rapid advancements at his work. He was very ambitious and hardworking. After getting his first salaried position, he worked long hours to do his best at learning all his new duties and responsibilities. He learned things quickly. For a guy who didn't graduate from high school, this seemed remarkable to me. After fifteen years my dad became superintendent of the largest and most productive department of his plant. He was doing so well that we bought a brand-new two-story, five-bedroom house in our neighborhood. It was on a choice corner lot right across the street from the school.

We moved in when I was about sixteen, and life started to move like we were in fast-forward. My dad bought a series of fancy cars, getting bored quickly with each one. Then he bought us a Doughboy swimming pool and everything that went with it. My dad was near the top of his world, and we all shared in that feeling. I became quite cocky in many ways. Nothing made me more popular than the fact that I worked in a grocery store and had access to beer. At first I would stash beer behind the store and sneak the money for it into the cash register. No one knew any better. I would buy only enough for myself and my closest friends, and they would share in the cost. After a while, I started selling it at a profit to other kids I was only acquainted with. Soon I was selling as many as ten cases of beer a weekend. Somehow I always found ways to pay the owners covertly.

Then, in the summer before my senior year, one of the girls I was going steady with got pregnant. This was a problem for more than the obvious reasons. Jane's father had long before forbidden her to see me, but we had been sneaking around anyway. He hadn't even given me a chance to meet him. All he had to know was that I had a Spanish surname; therefore I must have been the son of a "grape picker," to use his words. When I found out Jane was pregnant, I decided that I would accept the responsibility and marry her. Although I was seeing other girls, Jane was the one I saw the most and had the most fun with. The idea of being married to her was not uncomfortable. She was tiny, perhaps four feet eleven inches, about ninety pounds, and blond with bright blue eyes. She did well in school without really trying hard. What really stood out about her, though, was her personality. She had a wonderful sense of humor and a very good heart; she was warm and kind to everyone. It was difficult, however, for me to see us having a life together because of her father. I went to my parents with my problem, and they supported my decision to marry Jane. But when I approached her father with my intentions, he exploded into a rage. If not for the screen door between us, I think he would have hit me. He called me an animal and several other names that escape me now. He did not want me to marry his daughter or father a grandchild for him. Instead he insisted Jane have an illegal abortion. She acquiesced but with one condition: that she be allowed to see me freely and openly. He agreed and for a while tried to get to know me on a superficial level. When he found out I played baseball, he was somewhat impressed. In fact, baseball was the only thing we ever really talked about. He would read the box scores in the newspaper and say, "I noticed you got a couple of hits in your last game." I would reply, "Yes, sir," and that would be it. I continued to see Jane until I went into the marines, but I never got along any better with her father.

During the winter of 1967–68, my family's troubles started to come to a head. Our descent from the American dream began with the loss of my father's job.

My dad's plant had a Christmas party and awards banquet every year. That year, the plant manager was retiring and his successor was to be announced at the party. Of course everyone already knew to whom the job had gone, and it was not my dad. He had been hopeful that he would get the job; he felt he should get the job. But his rival, from another department, had a college education while my dad had not even graduated from high school. He became almost paralyzed with bitterness. That job would have been his crowning achievement. It was as far as he could have gone at his plant, and it was all that he wanted. Not getting it destroyed him.

My father had the habit of getting very drunk at company functions; this Christmas party was no different. From how my mother tells it, the announcement about the new plant manager had been made and several people were giving speeches about how wonderful the new boss would be. Apparently my father was grumbling to himself so loudly that the emcee invited him to stand and speak. Boy, did he speak. As everyone sat in amazement, my dad went on about what a jerk and kiss-ass the new manager was. If it was not for my dad covering for the new boss at crucial times, he would have been fired long ago. My dad also berated everyone who was kissing ass that night and criticized the company for their decision. He called them racists. When he was done, he and Mother stormed out. The next morning he was so ashamed and humiliated that he went to work only long enough to resign. After what he had said, the bosses did not argue. After fifteen years with one company, he was unemployed. From then on he never stayed anywhere long enough to work his way back up, and as his alcoholism progressed, it increasingly affected his working life.

I had to start thinking about what I was going to do when I graduated from high school. To everyone's surprise, I would be graduating. Despite all my fighting, boozing, and getting kicked out of the house six months earlier for wild parties, I had done just enough in school to get by. Because my parents did not graduate from high school, they assumed that anyone who did could choose whether or not to attend college. My mom had high hopes for me in the aftermath of what had happened to my dad. She was eager to hear what my school counselor, who had called for a meeting, would say about my options.

"Well, it looks like John is going to graduate in June after all," the counselor said. "It was a good idea for him to have attended summer school, especially this last summer. So what do you plan to do with yourself after graduation, John?"

My mother said, "We were hoping that John could go to college. What do you think?"

"That's not a realistic option for John, Mrs. Ramirez. His grades aren't good enough to be accepted into college."

"We were hoping he could start out at Foothill, where he could get in regardless of his present grades."

"Mrs. Ramirez, it's unfair to put such expectations on John. He would have a very difficult time of it even on the junior college level. Not everyone is suited for college, Mrs. Ramirez. John has other options. Have you considered vocational training in a trade?"

"Yes, but we're afraid he might get drafted if he just goes to work."

I lost my patience. "Oh, Mom!" I said. "Stop it! Stop trying to protect me!" I turned to my counselor. "Look, I've been out on my own for the last six months now. I'm able to make my own decisions. What are my chances of being drafted?"

"It is true, John, the chances are very good that you could be drafted within this year if you go to work in June. Have you considered enlisting? If you enlist, perhaps you can choose a line of training that is noncombative."

I did what I had known I would do for four years—go to

war. The war was not going away; in fact, at this point, Tet 1968, the war in Vietnam had reached an intensity level that scared and surprised everyone. The North Vietnamese were fighting back! How dare they! Guys I knew who had graduated or dropped out of school were there or already back. Many of my peers were making plans on how to evade the war, and almost none of my closest friends even considered volunteering, let alone allowing themselves to be drafted. In fact, none of my friends ever did go. The guys who ended up being drafted or volunteering were guys I knew casually, guys I had sold beer to or with whom I had fought — hard guys. No jocks, nerds, or brains. I didn't really know the other guys from the area that went to war, even though I was more like them than I ever knew. I had been fighting who I really was.

The prospect of waiting to be drafted did not go well with my nature. The fantasy of marrying a smart, pretty, blond, white girl was short-lived. Going to college, according to my counselor, was out of the question. I quit my job at the grocery store when the men who had hired me sold it. And I had been fired from a post office job for telling my boss to perform an impossible sexual act on himself. There was no escaping the inevitable. I felt compelled to enlist because it was my duty and obligation as a man to "do my part." It seemed natural. I was aware of the political struggle in our own country over the righteousness of the war. I took the side I believed was the right one.

I was eighteen years old and needed no permission from my parents to enlist in the Marine Corps. I entered a six-month early enlistment program, which meant I would get six months off my total enlistment at the end. I was scheduled to be inducted on June 24, 1968, eleven days after I graduated from high school, four days before my nineteenth birthday. To borrow a fellow veteran's explanation, "I joined the Marine Corps for all the usual dumb reasons." Like the Marine Corps being the best and most difficult test of manhood, for the tradition of *Semper Fidelis,* for the glory and honor of being a marine like John Wayne, whom I had watched land in the *Sands of Iwo Jima* so many times.

I think the recruiter would have promised me I could play baseball my whole enlistment if I had asked. Recruiters lie a lot and are never made to account for their deceit. Mine told me that if I wanted to cash in on full VA benefits after my enlistment, I would have to enlist for four years, the maximum. He said that if I enlisted for three years, I would only get partial benefits. (Later I found out that the Marine Corps also offered two-year enlistments, which the recruiter neglected to tell me.) My recruiter lied about the VA benefits, too. Even if you ended up doing eighteen months of a two-year enlistment and got out six months early, you would still receive the same benefits as the enlistee who signed up for four years. My recruiter also promised I would receive special training in law enforcement. It never happened.

In the end, I got *had.* I enlisted for four years.

My parents were stunned. At first they blamed each other for my actions. Then my father started in on me about how stupid my decision was and how maybe I could get out of it. My mother babbled on about how kids like me were the ones getting killed, repeating, "Oh, my God," over and over again. I was especially upset by my father's reaction—I had expected him to be proud of me.

It actually did not take long for them to accept it. I think they thought I would back out at the last moment, because they didn't get anxious again until I graduated. I played varsity baseball that spring and also Senior Babe Ruth League. My team won the league that year, and my dad was asked to accept an award in my absence after the season was over. He later wrote a rare letter to me saying how moved he was by what my coach and friends had said about me at the awards dinner. In a coded sort of way, he gave me some due.

Before I left, my great-grandmother, Angelita Bautista Cortez, asked to see me. She was in a convalescent home. My mother had told her I was leaving for the war. Angelita believed we would not see each other again, but she had a far more profound purpose for our visit. She wanted to give me something, a religious token made of green felt with a picture of the Virgin Mary on it. It was about five inches tall and three inches wide and hung on a string. She asked that we say a few prayers together, then she blessed the token and put it around my neck and kissed me and blessed me. She made my mother promise that she would take me to Mexico City on a pilgrimage to the Virgin of Guadalupe shrine to give thanks for my safe return. My mother agreed, and so did I.

This experience was so odd for me because I had not given much thought to religion or God since Grandma Ramirez's death years earlier. And I felt the kind of closeness with my great-grandmother that I had only shared with my grandma Ramirez. Under ordinary circumstances Angelita just didn't allow it. I was moved and scared for Angelita and for myself. She was kind and warm to me for what must have been more than an hour. I was in shock, and so was my mother.

On our way home my mother and I were silent. When we got there, my mother said, "We promised to go on the pilgrimage if you come back. We really must go, or you'll have bad luck the rest of your life."

"Sure, sure, Mom — I'll go."

Two

BOOT CAMP

I stepped off the bus at boot camp, and within the first ten minutes I knew that I was in for a long twelve weeks. The drill instructor who met our bus at the Marine Corps depot in San Diego was Sergeant King. He was a black man, about five-ten or five-eleven, with a lean body and a face so young, it was almost boyish. If it were not for his intensely stern expression and commanding voice, one would have thought he was the same age as his recruits.

He began yelling before we were even off the bus. After getting us lined up, he walked up and down the rows of young men standing at attention in our civilian clothes, checking us out and sometimes stopping in front of someone to stare. He told us what a bunch of losers we were and how he had his work cut out for him. He told us how important boot camp was and the purpose. He told us if he did his job correctly and effectively, it would save lives. He told us how proud he was to be a successful drill instructor and that he would not tolerate losers who ruined his reputation. He would form "eighty soft, weak, and stupid punks" into "men." Besides names like maggots and scum, he called us ladies and girls as if this were some kind of an insult. He said after he got through with us, we eighty individuals would be transformed into one single-minded unit. This unit would make one single sound when marching, not two or three, but one sound. He told us what our physical training, or PT, regimen was and how rigorous it would be. At that moment I could not help but smile. I was not scared or intimidated by the threats of hard physical work. In fact, I welcomed it. Even though it was nighttime and I was in the third row, Sergeant King spotted my smirking face. With lightning speed he lunged past the other recruits to get to me. He grabbed me by the throat before I knew what was happening. I was totally taken by surprise — it had happened so fast. Although I was scared, I vividly recall being impressed with Sergeant King's prowess, even at that very instant. He put his face right into mine, spraying me with his saliva as he yelled at me. He had pegged me right off as being cocky and told me so. He called me names and threatened to do everything within his power to break my will, destroy my confidence, and force me to conform or drive me out of his platoon and the Marine Corps. He was determined to take that smirk off my face, and for at least the next two weeks he did. For the next two weeks exactly. I remember it like it was yesterday — there would not be one day Sergeant King did not put hands on me.

On the twelfth or thirteenth day I had just gone to bed when I realized that I had gotten through the entire day without being singled out for punishment or abuse. Just as I began to feel pleased with myself, Sergeant King came crashing into the barracks. He came right to my rack (sleeping cot), where I was already getting out to stand at attention. He got up in my face and with an evil look said, "So you probably thought I forgot about you today, didn't you, Ramirez?" It was uncanny the way he seemed to know the very instant I had started to feel comfortable, as if he were letting me know I would never be allowed to feel comfortable. He ordered me outside with only my underwear on. It was dark; only the floodlights lit each hut entrance. Sergeant King had prepared a patch of mud next to his hut. He ordered me into this pit and made me do push-ups, sit-ups, and squat thrusts until I couldn't do anymore. He then ordered me back to bed without changing my clothes. I was humiliated. The next morning I was punished again for having gone to bed with muddy clothes. Then I was made to do push-ups on my knuckles, which were still caked with mud from the night before. I was ordered to wash my clothes on my own time that night, the time usually assigned for letter writing.

I seriously gave thought to deserting. I even had a plan, and if a friend hadn't convinced me not to, I would have. Nothing in my life to this point had been as demanding as this physical and psychological torture.

My own personal nightmare with Sergeant King ended after fourteen days. I'll never forget it. In the darkness of our hut, while we were all lying in bed, my fellow platoon members finally showed their support: "Way to go, Ramirez. You made it." "You're going to make it, guy." "Nice going, man." I was so choked up. I *was* going to make it. I think I had problems with drill because I had trouble concentrating on the commands. To this day I am still not sure why, but sometimes it felt like I wasn't hearing the commands as clearly as the others. The problem felt like school problems I had had in the past — a problem with concentration. At any rate, I came very close to being gang banged — beaten up by the rest of the platoon because everyone was punished when one member performed poorly — but a friend of mine, Paul Graff, talked our fellow recruits out of it.

I would not have made it without Paul. He and I had known each other before the Marine Corps, but we weren't friends, and we didn't even go to the same school: Paul went to a rival high school. We had played football and baseball against each other. In fact, in a football game a few years before I was personally responsible for Paul scoring a ninety-plus-yard touchdown. We saw each other again during baseball season. Once he even remarked how much he had enjoyed his touchdown. We had yet another connection. Unknown to us until we met and talked again at the induction center on our way to boot camp, we had dated sisters: he had gone steady with my former girlfriend's older sister. Our rivalry evaporated in that instant. Not surprising, considering where we were going. The friendship was more of a salvation to me than him. Besides keeping me from being beaten up, he gave me encouragement when my spirits were low. With a lot of support from Paul, I got through those first two weeks and even finally got in sync with the drill demands. And Sergeant King focused his wrath in other directions.

A frail young man who had been dropped from his original platoon because he could not hack it was assigned to our group during rifle training. Sergeant King immediately started in on him, determined to get rid of him before he got stuck with him. One morning within that first week at the rifle range the recruit was taken away in an ambulance, unconscious. We all knew what had happened because we had heard every blow, scream, and moan. Our sleeping arrangement at the rifle range was different than at San Diego Recruit Depot: all eighty of us slept in one large barracks with the drill instructor's quarters in the middle of the room. It was not unusual for Sergeant King or any of our other drill instructors to take a recruit into their hut or quarters to beat and torture him. But this time was different. As familiar as we were with Sergeant King's psychotic episodes, this was close to murder. And although we listened to the beating going on most of the night, none of us did anything about it.

Sergeant King's immediate superior, Gunnery Sergeant Olsen, gathered us all together a few days after to tell us there would be an investigation regarding the recruit's injuries. Gunny Olsen was a huge, bearlike man who was also black.

There were times when he would abuse us, either as a group or individually, but he had boundaries and controlled himself, as did our other two drill instructors. Sergeant King was totally unpredictable, with little or no conscience about what he did. Gunny Olsen told us that what had happened was a mistake and regrettable but added that it would be an even bigger mistake to misunderstand what had happened. He gave us a long lecture about Sergeant King's commitment to producing the finest and best marines in the corps, and how sometimes this endeavor called for extreme measures and actions. He told us that in the next week we would be asked questions regarding the beating. He instructed us how to answer the questions without lying or implicating Sergeant King. All during Gunny Olsen's lecture, Sergeant King was pacing nervously up and down in our ranks, sometimes stopping in front of someone just to glare. Gunny Olsen told us that if anything happened to Sergeant King as a result of the investigation, he and the other drill instructors would take serious offense and revenge.

We talked among ourselves about finally being able to get rid of this maniac. But we always came to the same self-preserving conclusion — just five more weeks and we would be gone. And after all, we understood the recruit would recover and be medically discharged because of his injuries. The investigation started the very next day. The investigating officers randomly took a group or an individual aside to ask questions. All this was done within plain view of our drill instructors. At no time were we questioned in private or offered anonymity. The whole incident passed without any further attention, and Sergeant King kept right on terrorizing the weak recruits.

For what it's worth, our platoon, 3025, achieved the Distinction of Honor Platoon. All but three out of eighty who started with the platoon graduated. Although I felt some degree of pride in making it through this ordeal, my prevailing feelings were of humility and anger. I vowed to myself that I would kill Sergeant King if I ever saw him again.

My mother and sister Evie surprised me with a visit on graduation day. They said my father was supposed to have come but got drunk. I was disappointed. I was prouder of my graduation from boot camp than of anything else I'd ever accomplished — even graduation from high school, which really seemed like a mistake. At my high school graduation I kept expecting someone to come and say an error had been made and that I couldn't really graduate. At my graduation from boot camp I had no such feeling — I knew I had earned it.

The day after graduation we were transported to Camp Pendleton for infantry training regiment, or ITR. Most of us were scattered throughout different training units. Paul was in a completely different regiment, but we tried to stay in contact. I made a few friends, but I also started to make a few enemies.

Unlike in my boot camp platoon, there were a lot more Chicanos in my ITR company. Almost immediately a couple of these guys started making fun of my lack of accent and propensity to befriend white guys. They were truly angry that I didn't sound like them. My loudest and most annoying Chicano antagonizer would choose moments when a lot of guys were around (so as not to get himself hurt) and repeatedly call me "Mexican." "Hey, Mexican. You Mexican or what?" as if the word *Mexican* were some kind of insult. At first I was puzzled. Why did he think I would be insulted by what I was? My friends told me to ignore him, that it was not worth getting into trouble over. But it was getting to me. I had started to plan how I would corner this little punk and pound him when two Mexican guys, fairly recent immigrants, approached me: "We don't understand why Chicanos fight this way with each other. Aren't we all on the same side? Aren't we all marines?" Their questions — so genuine and sincere — helped me realize I had a far more important duty to perform than to be distracted by the childish behavior. I decided to ignore my antagonizers and went on with my training.

The seriousness of where I was going and what I was going to do took over my consciousness. I thought of little else. We spent most of our time in forced marching with all of our gear—packs, weapons, and ammo—for long distances. We were also schooled in the use of several different weapons. Our next phase of training was called basic infantry training specialty, or BITS. BITS was a much smaller training unit than ITR. We were 0351, or antitank men. We received training with the 106 recoilless rifle, the 3.5 rocket launcher, and demolitions. There were moments during this training when I felt like I was in boot camp again, and it wasn't supposed to be that way. I was depressed the entire time and, although I did well in my training scores, I never seemed to achieve emotional balance. It was as if I were standing outside myself, a different part of myself watching me sheepishly take the abuse, scolding, Why don't you do something? What's wrong with you?

During the next phase of training, the two weeks before going to Vietnam, we were able to wander about the base on our free time and even leave the base on the few weekends we had left. It was the first time since joining the corps that I felt like a regular marine and not just a recruit. I felt like I had just gotten out of prison.

On my first weekend of freedom, I was watching some guys playing football at one of the fields on the base and noticed someone familiar running a touchdown. It was Paul Graff, my friend from boot camp. I was very happy to see him. I had made one or two other friends since, but my friendship with Paul was special. We talked about our training experiences since boot camp and our anticipation about Vietnam. As always he was upbeat, lighthearted, and enthusiastic. He invited me to play football the next day, Sunday. I accepted and in turn invited him to go out on the town with me and some other guys to get drunk and maybe get a Marine Corps tattoo. Paul laughed at this idea and said, "No, thanks. I don't want the Marine Corps stamped on me for the rest of my life. Besides, I don't feel like getting drunk." I said I'd see him the next day at the field. He cracked that huge infectious smile of his and said, "Don't get too drunk, or I might just run two touchdowns across your face tomorrow."

"Sure, sure. See you tomorrow," I said.

That night I walked the streets of Oceanside with three other guys, stopping at various bars, looking for girls, and building up the courage to get tattooed at one of the many parlors. The idea of finding girls was pretty absurd because marines probably outnumbered the women in town twenty to one. Recruits paraded up and down the streets looking for action but only saw other recruits. I never did get drunk that night. Nor did I get a tattoo, although the rest of the guys I was with did. Paul's wisdom prevailed.

The next day we got together to play football. We had been playing for about twenty minutes when Paul broke his leg. He was so upset, he cried, but not because of the pain. He was devastated over being delayed in his training and eventual departure for Vietnam, and, of course, in his leave home somewhere in between training and Vietnam. Although I was surprised to see him so emotional, I understood. Especially in Paul's case — to get this far and not finish with his graduating class. It's crazy to most sane people, but along with the desire to finish training, most of us were anxious to get on with the reason we were there — to fight and maybe die in Vietnam. Waiting for one's destiny is far more painful than meeting it.

Watching Paul being taken away by ambulance was an image that would stay with me for the rest of my life. I realized at that moment that finding and losing friends would be a part of this experience. On the one hand, I was happy for him. Maybe he got lucky breaking his leg; maybe by the time he healed, the war would wind down or even end. On the other hand, I was disappointed for him and myself because now we would not be leaving for Okinawa and Vietnam together. As the ambulance drove away I wondered if I'd ever see him again.

Staging battalion lasted one more week, then it was home for a short ten-day leave. The leave was depressing. A lot had changed at home. My father had not been able to find another job making the kind of money he had before. My parents were forced to give up the dream house they had purchased four years earlier and were now renting a house in Palo Alto. After all those years building a certain lifestyle — it was a shock to me to see my family in such a bad state. I felt some guilt for leaving. Maybe if I hadn't left, I could have helped them keep the house by going to work instead. My parents were ashamed of how their situation had deteriorated. They acted as if they had let me down. I had known a lot had changed, but they had been careful to keep the details from me while I was away. They didn't even have the same furniture or cars. The rented house was old but comfortable, in a nice older neighborhood but much smaller than we were used to. I hardly saw my sister Evelyn — she was always out and carrying on with her friends. My mother was very depressed and nervous. My father was not working at the time, and when he wasn't looking for work, he was usually drinking. He hardly talked to me when I was there. He was aloof and seemed in another world.

I went out a few times with my friends, but I didn't have much fun. It felt so much like a waste of time, although I did have one very memorable night just before I left. Several of us drove to Santa Cruz for a night beach party. On our way there, they talked me into trying some pot, which was now a normal part of their partying. In fact, as the night progressed I found out they were using other drugs, too. Before I went to boot camp, only a few of my friends smoked pot, let alone used other drugs. That night my willingness to try pot was somewhat of a shock to my friends as they had remembered how I reacted the first time I found out they were smoking it.

Back when I was sharing an apartment with three of my friends, I went looking for rent money in one of their sport coats. I discovered a bag of marijuana instead. Shocked, scared, and angry, I took the "evil weed" outside and buried it! When my roommates came home and asked about it, I told them I was scared I would go to jail for having it in the house. "Okay, fine. Where did you bury it?" Because it was dark outside when I buried it, I wasn't sure where it was. We looked for a long time — until the landlord questioned why we were digging up the yard. We never did find it. Man, were they mad at me! Twenty dollars' worth was a lot of pot in those days.

But on that night we drove to Santa Cruz, my attitude had changed. "Oh, well. Why the fuck not! I could be dead in a month or two." I not only smoked pot that night, I also took LSD. All my friends were totally bewildered by this behavior. Although the experience was new for me and my consciousness seemed to be floating at times, I at least seemed to have control of it. I found it to be interesting, but I was not sure if I liked it. Although my mind was being altered in ways I had never experienced before, it did not seem all that different from how I had been feeling since coming home. The experience showed me how much I had changed. Even before I smoked the pot and ate the acid, I felt like I was outside my body, watching myself interact with my family and friends and having a dialogue with myself. "Who are these people? I don't understand what they are saying. Everybody is so different. What is happening? I don't belong here anymore." The drugs only seemed to intensify the way I already felt.

The ride home through the canyon felt like I was free falling down a dark, spiraling tube. I kept staring intently out the window, trying to see something other than my own reflection because I didn't like what I saw. It didn't look like me. The person I saw was laughing at me and whispering, "You're dead, man. You're dead, man," over and over. Then suddenly I was home, or at least what my family now called home. My friends seemed relieved as they dropped me off. I watched them drive off, knowing I would never see them again, but it felt okay.

When I walked in the house, my dad was still awake, watching *The Tonight Show Starring Johnny Carson*. He was waiting up for me, I suppose. I think he wanted to talk, but I couldn't and didn't. "I'm going to bed now, Dad."

He called me back into the living room and asked, "Are you all right?"

"Sure, I'm just tired." The wall in front of me was filled with little TV screens like a checkerboard, with Johnny Carson's face on each one of them. "I'm not really okay," I said to myself, and went to bed.

At that time in my life I had no sense of control, no idea of making plans or having any ability to determine my own future. Things happened to me and I reacted to them. I didn't have a consciousness built out of education or experience that could provide a larger sense of meaning to the events happening to me. I just lived one day at a time, hoping for the best, fearing the worst, and just getting on with it.

The next day I left for Camp Pendleton. When I arrived, I was told we would be leaving in three days. It was approximately November 13, 1968. I was technically still in 9th Staging Battalion Unit, but we were no longer training. We were allowed to wander about the base during the day and into town at night. One afternoon while on my way to the post exchange, or PX, I saw a familiar guy walking out. He really stood out from the rest of us. His fatigues, cap, and boots were "salty," or worn and ragged. It was obvious that he had just arrived home from Vietnam. As he got closer to me I realized he was an old enemy from high school. I wasn't sure how to act at first. We made eye contact at the same time and broke into smiles. Jim was five-ten, blond, green eyed, and thin. His friends had been car guys and hard guys. Because I was a jock, my friends and I would occasionally fight with them, but for the most part we stayed away from each other. Here, though, we talked as if we were long lost friends. He was very generous with his time and information about what it was like "in-country." He even invited me to go out that night with him to party and talk more about "Nam." I was grateful and in awe of him.

It turned out to be a strange and eerie night. Jim rented a car, then we bought whiskey and beer and went to a drive-in movie. Jim also had some pot that we shared. I do not even remember what the movie was about. Jim did most of the talking. The drunker he got, the deeper he would go down into his heart. After a while, as if coming up for air, he stopped and said, "Oh, I'm sorry. I hope I'm not scaring you. It's just that I feel like I'm still there sometimes. It's still hard for me to believe I'm home." He was right. I was getting scared. He had explained that it was so different than he was led to believe, that the enemy was fierce and formidable. He talked about near death experiences, losing friends, and killing people and not knowing how to deal with the feelings. He would stop and just stare out the driver's side window, thinking. Finally and suddenly he stopped talking. "Hey, don't worry. You'll make it. Maybe you'll get lucky and get noncombat duty." He wanted to leave then.

Why wasn't he happier that he had made it home alive? He was haunted, and that got to me more than anything.

Combat

A man
spoke to me in empty words
of the year in which his life ended.
Trapped at nineteen,
unable to grow beyond it,
fifteen years passed for the rest of us
but he had died without
knowing it at the time;
even though he burned his fatigues
(and regretted it later)
threw his medals at the White House,
grew his hair out long,
the external changes could not revive
the comatose spirit inside
the aging body.
He could not tell me
the truth about that year
and the truth of the other years
depend on the truth of it.
He could not tell me, he said,
because I was not there.
So I must be punished, as an outsider,
by silence forever.
He could tell me stories,
but he could not tell me the truth.
You saw the truth, he said,
on the six o'clock news.

But I remember
Walter Cronkite in the jungle
in the same frame as I remember
Ben Gazzara in the desert;
"Combat," the news, they were the same
in the twelve-year-old eyes
that watched the living room screen.

So the man and I put our hands together,
and only skin touches.

Renny Christopher

Part Two

DURING

Three

WAR STORIES

I arrived in Vietnam on November 29, 1968, at a military airfield in Da Nang. I expected there to be a lot of shooting and fighting going on, but there wasn't. They simply loaded us onto some waiting helicopters. The choppers took us out to sea, then landed on what looked like a very small aircraft carrier. None of us had any idea what was going on.

We were told we were being assigned to a BLT (battalion landing team), BLT 2/26 (2nd Battalion, 26th Marine Regiment). We all knew we were going to the 26th Marines before we left our last stop-off point in Okinawa. While in Okinawa, we had crossed paths with marines on their way home. Some of them warned us about being assigned to 9th or 26th Marines, that both those units were experiencing combat and sustaining high rates of casualties. Those of us who were going to the 9th or 26th hoped that most of what we were hearing was hazing, but from the looks of those who were returning from the 9th and 26th, we had good reason to believe them, so this assignment caused us some anxiety.

I spent two days on the ship (the USS *Okinawa* helicopter assault ship) and then went on to the first three days of my first combat operation. This particular operation was named Bold Mariner. Its purpose was to search and destroy. This means that a particular group of hamlets (three in this case, in the northwest corner of Quang Tri Province) had supposedly been discovered as or were suspected to be occupied by Vietcong (VC) sympathizers and supporters. Based on this intelligence, we were ordered to round up all the people we could find; herd them into choppers for "relocation," destroy all shelters, supplies (food and building supplies), and any other resources; then evacuate ourselves so the air force could spray defoliant over the entire area.

The logic behind the U.S. military's policy was that the VC's ability to conduct a successful guerrilla war was dependent on hamlets like these for hiding underground supplies (food and ammo), medical treatment, and information. In other words, the hamlet provided a base camp of operation. In destroying the resources and "relocating" the people, supposedly we would be destroying a VC base camp.

This was my first real combat operation; most of what I remember is as clear to me as if it happened yesterday. The destruction that we wreaked on those people, so quickly, overawed me. Some of the guys were enjoying it, but as I watched the mass destruction, the explosions, the fire, the smoke, all I could do was look at it, amazed by the level of havoc we were causing, and think, "Oh, fuck!"

We spent all of the first day rounding up people and herding them into helicopters. The next day we spent burning houses and resources, searching out tunnels, then blowing up their entrances. I had made the mistake of telling my squad leader, Corporal Jensen, that I had been trained in the use of demolitions. That led to the following exchange.

"Hey, Ramirez. You're assigned to assist the demo man. Go get some C-4 from battalion. Then go help the demos out," Jensen said.

"What was that?"

"You heard me."

"If you mean help them set charges, okay. But if you mean go down into the tunnels, no! I'm not going to do that! I don't want to be a tunnel rat!"

"The hell you're not!"

"Look, Jensen. I know you don't like me, and I also know I don't *have* to do 'tunnel rat' work by order, and I'm not going to volunteer! You're going to have to kick my ass, and I'm frankly welcoming the chance to kick yours!"

"You're going to be a problem, aren't you? Well, we'll settle this later. Just set charges, then, and don't give those demos any problems 'cause they'll take no shit from a 'boot.'"

I went over to the demo leader. "I was sent to help you guys set charges. I've got C-4 and blasting caps. Where do you want me to start?"

The demo leader told me, "I'm busy right now! Just go over where those guys are and watch for now."

I spent most of that afternoon blowing up tunnel entrances. So far, we hadn't encountered any resistance to what we were doing. We were freely performing our assignment. I didn't feel much like a warrior. So far, what I was experiencing was not at all what I had expected. It wasn't anything like what John Wayne did in *Sands of Iowa Jima*. It didn't seem like a war at all — just like we were tearing apart the lives and property of ordinary people. This was my introduction to the war that I had expected to constitute a test of manhood, an opportunity for honor and glory. I was confused. Nothing was matching up to what I was trained to expect.

That first day coming in had started out more in line with what I expected because we had *then* met with resistance. As our chopper was coming in, we were being shot at but could not see where the fire was coming from. The crew chief said that the pilot would not land because, "It's the ship that they're after." He said we would have to jump when he said so.

After we jumped (not all at the same time), we were safe,

because it *was* the ship they were after. Up to the end of the day we burned the hamlet, that was the extent of our contact with resistance.

But something else that happened earlier on that first day, when our squad was part of the security for herding the villagers into choppers for relocation, had given me my first misgivings about the conduct of the war. As the column of Vietnamese people passed us in single file, some of our guys were pushing and kicking people along, sometimes jabbing the muzzle of their rifles into the people's ribs or up their rear ends.

Most of the guys who were doing these things had been "in-country" longer than most of us boots. It seemed to be all right with Jensen because he was the chief antagonizer. Some of the boots joined in, although hesitantly, and some, like me, just guarded the prisoners. It was during this process that the image of Nazis from World War II movies first entered my head. I didn't want to see it that way, but while I was standing guard over this line of people, I felt terrible, because this wasn't anything like my idea of what war would be: armed men facing each other is combat. Instead here I was watching Americans abuse civilians who they were removing from their homes. I tried not to keep seeing those movie images of Nazi troops herding Jewish people down streets where they had lived, pushing and kicking them as they passed, but I couldn't keep them away.

It was all real, I kept realizing, both what was happening in front of me and what I was seeing in my head. Those images were from actual film footage I remembered seeing on television while I was growing up. And what I was a part of was real also, making it difficult for me to separate my own sense of what was right and wrong from what I was helping to do. Nothing in my training, my education, nothing at all in my past prepared me for the reality of this war I had entered into.

I began to realize that I hadn't really known anything at all about the war before I arrived in the middle of it.

Later that evening we were surveying the damage we had done. I was sitting on a grassy knoll with some other marines, talking, smoking cigarettes, watching the three hamlets burn, wondering what good it would do. I saw Jensen walking toward me, and I couldn't help thinking how much I disliked him. The sight of him gave me the creeps. I felt unlucky to have ended up with him as my squad leader.

Jensen was from the Southwest. He had been in Vietnam almost eleven months, with two more or so to go. Jensen was a short-timer. Short-timers were guys who had three months or less left of their tours of duty. I don't know what he had been like before he got to Vietnam, but it didn't take long for me to learn about him and his modus operandi.

In a word, he was just plain *mean*. He hated everybody: intellectual whites, boots, "pickups" (from other units), officers, truck drivers, helicopter pilots, and especially people of color — he was a bigot pure and simple. Being a short-timer added to his uptightness. He was growing increasingly paranoid that he might not make it home. It caused me to feel that I had become expendable to his survival. Others like me felt the same.

Jensen said, "Ramirez. You're going to be with me and Smith for hole watch tonight. Follow me."

The hole was our dug-in position on our nightly line or perimeter of defense. Someone was always on guard or watch there while the others slept. The more guys to a hole, the more sleep you got. At this hole tonight, it would be me, Jensen, and his right-hand man, Smith.

Smith was already at our nighttime position. He and Jensen had made themselves at home, utilizing what remained of a Vietnamese hootch, a small thatched hut. Smith and Jensen spent about an hour chasing and catching three chickens that they would keep alive until it suited them to eat them. I wasn't interested in any of it.

Jensen was called up the line to the command post (CP), leaving me alone with Smith. Smith tried to explain Jensen's attitude to me by saying how much they had gone through together and how they had been betrayed by Vietnamese villagers. I wouldn't listen. I was determined not to trust either one of them.

Jensen came back with a Vietnamese boy. The boy was about thirteen years old. He was wearing white pajamas, not the more common black pajamas we were accustomed to seeing. Jensen was pushing him along with his hands tied. "Look what *we* got, Smith. The CO [commanding officer] wants us to watch the little slope overnight. The backup unit found him trying to hide out till we left. Ramirez, you got first and fourth watch. Don't untie or feed the slope! Understand?"

"Yeah, yeah, sure," I said, mumbling, "motherfucker!"

"What's that you said?"

"Oh, nothing, nothing at all, Corporal."

Jensen and Smith fell right to sleep. They had had a long day burning and looting.

I said to the boy, "You speak English?" There was no response from him. Hmmm, I said to myself. The expression on this boy's face had not changed since I first made eye contact with him. His face was hard and taut. It seemed to be the face of an angry man rather than that of a thirteen-year-old boy. I couldn't help thinking, If this boy isn't a VC, he'll shortly become one. I also couldn't help noticing that he was not afraid of us.

After I knew Jensen and Smith were asleep, I opened a can of C-ration sliced peaches. I ate a couple of slices, then gestured to ask the boy if he wanted any. He defiantly shook his head no, but I could see he was hungry because his face had loosened when he saw the peaches, just ever so slightly.

How sad for him to be a prisoner in his own village, I

thought. I couldn't stand it any longer, so I untied him. Fear and confusion showed on the boy's face. I handed him the can of peaches and a fork, but this time he thought about it. He looked into the hootch, then looked around the area as if someone were watching in hiding, then took the peaches from my hand very gently.

He inhaled those peaches, not looking up once till he was finished. After he had eaten them, I thought he would smile or grin or say thank you, but he didn't. I was trying to talk to him, but my voice was causing Jensen to stir. It was making the boy nervous. I was nervous, too, so I stopped trying to talk to him since Jensen might wake up.

I didn't bother to retie his hands because I figured it would be okay while I was on watch, anyway. We just sat there, checking each other out. I lit a cigarette, hand cupping the tip so as not to attract sniper fire. The boy's eyes grew rounder when he saw the "cigs," so I offered him one. Just like magic, he smiled. He smiled the way a thirteen-year-old boy might smile when he got something he always wanted. I thought, How sad that this simple gesture would bring him back. He now seemed truly relaxed, almost secure. His face was happy. He made me happy, too.

Jensen woke up in a startled state. He must have been dreaming. "Hey, what the fuck's going on here!" He slapped the boy's face, knocking the cig out of his mouth. "Goddamn it, Ramirez! You're forcing me to take action against you if you don't knock off this shit of disobeying orders! I said no untying his hands, no food, no cigs, no nothing! Are you retarded or something?"

"I'm not retarded, and I don't really care what you do."

"Tie his fucking hands again and blindfold him this time."

I tied the boy up again, then blindfolded him. It was just as well. I couldn't look in his eyes anymore, anyway. I had gotten him to smile, then gotten him in trouble with Jensen. I felt guilty for getting him slapped.

The next morning Jensen took the boy back up to the CP, where he would be interrogated, then loaded up and "relocated" like the others had been.

While Jensen was gone, there had been some small arms fire in the distance. It sounded like ours. Jensen came running back, out of breath. He struggled to say, "You know that little gook kid we had here last night? That dumb shit started to run away when the choppers came, so we had to shoot him!"

"Was he armed?"

"No, no, of course not, you idiot!"

First I was shocked, then I was angry. He hadn't been armed. He had just been running away, and they'd killed him for running away like any normal kid would. I couldn't believe they didn't seem to feel anything about it. I actually felt sad for Jensen and Smith because they couldn't feel anymore.

I was appalled at Jensen's reaction to this tragedy, which he didn't see as a tragedy at all. I was so stunned, all that came to my mind was: Did that boy have a fighting chance, or was he gunned down in cold blood? I knew the answer to my question before I asked it, but I didn't want to hear it. I didn't know at the time how I would be influenced and changed forever by experiences like this one. I also didn't know at the time how much I would be changed after I'd been in this war as long as Smith and Jensen. In that moment it appeared that they had lost their sense of humanity and I had retained mine, but I had only been there for five days. I, too, would soon be less than sensitive.

Four

QUANG NAM PROVINCE, VIETNAM, JANUARY 1969

One That Died

You bet we'll soon forget the one that died;
he isn't welcome any more.
He could too easily take our place
for us to think about him
any longer than it takes
to sort his personal effects:
a pack of letters,
cigarettes,
photos and a wallet.
We'll keep the cigarettes;
divide them up among us.
His parents have no use for them,
and cigarettes are hard to get.

— W. D. Ehrhart

I was sure I would be one who would die tomorrow. I think I always believed that I was going to die in Vietnam, at least from 1964, the year I began worrying about having to eventually participate in the war.

I had already been through my first combat operation on quite a grand scale: thousands of troops, hundreds of helicopters, and even journalists. Even though I was a completely inexperienced marine, I thought the presence of the cameras and journalists was unusual. After all, John Wayne never had such "unnecessary" personnel around in his movies.

Not much happened to us in that operation. We took hardly any casualties ourselves. But we did inflict a great deal of hardship on the local villagers.

So far, I still did not feel I was doing what I was sent here to do—fight "communism." I had believed that fighting the spread of communism was an important thing, that it was America's duty to defend the free world, and so Americans had to make sacrifices in order to carry out a noble goal. But nothing we were doing here looked like fighting communism, so all that I had been brought up to value and deem important had been called into question. Even so, all I had were doubts. I didn't have any new ideas to replace the old ones. I continued to hope that things would get better, that the war would start to look like I had expected it to and it would suddenly all make sense again. All I could do was try to do as well as I could in each small situation, try not to become like Jensen, and just keep on going.

I knew we were moving on to a different kind of operation, one that I hoped would make more sense. We were going to be facing real, honest to God NVA (North Vietnamese army) soldiers, and we were scared. The NVA weren't guerrillas; they were a regular army, and I expected this to be a regular battle, not an action carried out against civilians. So even though I was scared, I thought I was finally going to see my expectations of the war fulfilled.

Early the day before we would be engaging the NVA, we were briefed about what we should expect. Our superiors said the battalion could expect to take "30 to 40 percent casualties." In other words, some of you are going to die tomorrow and some the next day, and then some more. And of course some of us might get lucky and only get wounded and sent home. That night we were treated to a steak dinner and all the beer we could drink instead of the usual C rations we ate.

As of yet, I had made no friends or buddies to speak of. There was no one I really liked. But that night I felt a need to find a friend. There was a large group of guys in the enlisted men's club, which was in a tent, drinking very quietly by candlelight. There was a group sitting outside their tent, quietly singing country songs to each other. Then there were men like me, walking around restlessly or sitting alone at their racks, restlessly writing letters or reading old ones. I saw a black marine I knew from our last assignment. He seemed friendly enough, so I approached him to talk. He was from the South, I think Florida, maybe. Tall, thin, with big round, sort of drooping eyes. He spoke softly and slowly, almost afraid to disturb the aura of death around us. I don't remember his name, but I liked him, and I think he liked me. He was sort of a new guy, I think three months in-country.

I was pumping him for information on what we could really expect the next day. I told him I was scared that I would die because of my lack of experience, since I'd only been there four weeks, and asked if he could point out someone in my platoon who had been around longer who I could talk to. Ever since I had arrived in-country, I had felt alone and unconnected to any sense of camaraderie. I'm sure we all thought we would be one of those who would die tomorrow.

My new friend said, "There is one guy you ought to know about. That's him over there." He pointed to a man standing facing a wooden partition used for showering. He was throwing a K-bar (a large knife) at the wooden partition.

My friend said, "That's Roberts. He's been here nine months now. He has a Purple Heart and a Bronze Star already. He's the 2nd Squad's squad leader. He don't talk much, but he's a real nice guy, likes to help new guys."

Roberts couldn't have been over nineteen years old. Not at all what I had expected. My preconception of the typical, seasoned, combat marine was more of the bull-faced, hardened but gentle type. Maybe you know the type. About thirty or thirty-five years old, ugly but handsome when he smiles. He doesn't speak well but doesn't have to because he's been in the

Marine Corps his whole adult life. His skin is tan and thick, almost leathery. You know he knows his shit just by looking in his eyes and listening to his voice. Somebody you could rely on in a pinch. Someone you'd want by your side when it counted.

No. Roberts wasn't anything like I had hoped for. Except that he had those eyes: the kind that had outgrown his heart and mind. They'd seen more than his nineteen years could sort out. But they were smart eyes, keen to survival, keen to the knowledge of the bush even if he'd only been there nine months. I could see he knew something that I needed to know by tomorrow morning.

Roberts was about five-eleven, thin, a very poor white kid from Illinois. We talked about our lives, my fears, his experiences, and the next day. He asked me why I wasn't asking my own squad leader these questions.

I said, "I don't trust or like him." In fact, I thought Jensen was a racist. Because Jensen was a short timer, that made me and everyone else expendable to him. He was useless and later proved to be so.

Roberts smiled and said he understood. He said that he and Jensen had been in the same squad together when he first came in-country.

Roberts's advice eased much of my tension and fear, but most of all I felt I had made a friend. Roberts's advice was in essence this: (1) Don't play the hero, (2) learn how to read a map and compass and learn how to use the radio, (3) don't follow or listen to dangerous fanatics, (4) and above all, do not underestimate the VC and NVA soldiers. Stay scared! His advice turned out to be the best I received from anyone.

The next morning the mood was still very sullen as we boarded the choppers. When we got to the landing zone (LZ), we were getting shot at as we were coming in. The pilot couldn't or didn't want to land, so he ordered us to jump from about ten feet up.

We regrouped as a unit in about ten minutes. Then there

was a calm for about thirty minutes as we proceeded in a long, stretched-out column of about two hundred men. Our squad was about fifty guys back from the point squad (the front of the column).

The column suddenly came to a halt. It didn't seem unusual at first. We didn't hear any gunfire. It was a long wait — maybe fifteen or twenty minutes. Our squad was called up to the front. As we passed the others on our way up no one said a word, or maybe they just didn't know anything. I started to get uneasy. It was so strange. No one told us what was going on. We just kept moving up to the front, passing other marines resting just as we had been doing earlier.

Then I could hear rifle fire — friendly and enemy. All of a sudden we came around a bend in the trail our marching had made, and there on the ground were two men in body bags, lying dead with only their boots sticking out. I could not breathe. Even though I knew I was in a combat zone, it seemed as though when we turned that bend, we walked through a door, then closed it behind us so as not to disturb anyone following us. The sound of the rifle fire also seemed to increase as we walked through the "door."

A sergeant yelled at us to follow him farther up. I didn't recognize him, but he sort of looked and sounded like that ideal marine from my childhood imagination. So we followed him into a huge B-52 bomb crater. There was a lot of commotion. Guys were frantically talking into their radios for artillery support and medevac choppers. The sergeant seemed to be the only one in control of himself. As I jumped into the bomb crater I immediately noticed two more bodies in bags and our platoon commander, Lieutenant Crawford, being attended to by a corpsman (a navy enlisted man trained to give first aid and minor medical treatment). He was suffering from heatstroke. It looked as if they had been under siege for hours, but no more than thirty minutes could have passed since the column first stopped.

The lieutenant was useless, and for a moment so were we. All of us who were brought up from the rear were new guys. Here it was. This was it. Dead bodies, confusion, and some very determined men out in front of us trying with all their hearts to kill us, and they were succeeding. We were using the crater for cover. Out in front of us were two heavily fortified bunkers that were staggered and supporting each other. They looked like rats' nests you might see in the woods except bigger and they were very well camouflaged. I could see how the point of the column had walked between them without detecting them. The sergeant positioned us around the perimeter of the bomb crater and directed us to fire at the bunkers out in front. One of the bodies in the bomb crater with us seemed familiar — I mean, one of the pairs of boots sticking out seemed familiar. I kept staring at them while everyone else was shooting. The sergeant shouted at me to stop staring and start shooting, but I couldn't stop staring. Finally he came over to me and said, "What's the matter, Marine? Haven't you ever seen a dead body before?"

I said, "No, sir; I mean, yes, sir. But who is that? Is that Corporal Roberts, sir?"

He said, "Yes, young man. And if you don't start shooting right now, you are going to end up the same way! Now get your ass turned around and start shooting!"

I said, "Yes, sir." And I did. I mean, I started shooting.

Even while I was firing, I was thinking about my short friendship with Roberts and how terrible it felt to find him dead all of a sudden like that, and I decided on the spot I would not make any more friends if I could help it.

The guy next to me said he thought we might have knocked out one of the bunkers. There didn't appear to be any fire coming from the one to our right. The sergeant confirmed this and directed us to proceed against the bunker to our left. While we were returning fire, a first lieutenant came diving into our bomb crater with a radioman close behind him. I had never seen this lieutenant before. He was very excited and gung ho, asking the sergeant about our enemy and if we had made any attempt to assault the bunkers. The sergeant pointed at the dead bodies lying around and said, "Yeah, and there they are. There's one more out front." He pointed outside the bomb crater.

The lieutenant glared at the sergeant and the rest of us as if we were not doing our best. Then he looked us over, looking right into each man's eyes, scanning back and forth very quickly. His eyes intensely fixed on the guy to my right. Then he looked at me once more before he said to the other man, "You come with me." With that the guy and the radioman followed him out of the crater.

He was intent on making another assault. Just before they left, he said, "We're going to make an end-around move," using a football metaphor. It fit him since he looked like a football player, a big college jock type. Seconds later we heard a burst of automatic rifle fire, then screams. The sergeant just shook his head and said, "Stupid motherfucker," then looked at us very sternly and said, "I can see you're new meat. Watch out for those types, and don't move — they're probably dead, anyway. Just keep firing at that bunker." He didn't have to worry. I had no intention of going after them. When we popped up to fire back, I could see at least one of their bodies.

After it was all over, we could easily figure out what had happened to them. We discovered that these bunkers had what we called "spider holes," which leached out from them. Each bunker had about three of them. They were tunnels the NVA soldiers could go into, then pop up and surprise anyone who tried to sneak up on them. They had the lids, or hatch-type doors, camouflaged to blend in with the rest of the sur-face. They could pop up in front of you, behind you, or to the side, completely surprising an unsuspecting foe. This guy ap-parently popped up in front of the lieutenant, his radioman, and our guy. I never spoke to our man or knew his name. He was a boot, a new guy. It looked as simple as it sounded. One burst of automatic rifle fire had cut all three of them down.

Our guy, the boot, was like me and so many of us who were fighting that day, fresh off the "meat wagon." I didn't know him, but I will never forget that look on his face as he looked back at us when he left the crater, scared and reluctant. I will also never forget the sight of his new boots sticking out the bottom of the body bag. It could easily have been me.

After the lieutenant and the other two went out, whoever was in the two bunkers had killed eight of us, wounded eleven, and shot down two medevac choppers all in a span of about three hours. Now there was only one bunker left, and I couldn't help but wonder, Who are these men that they would fight with such determination?

Finally we heard a loud scream from the one remaining bunker. The sergeant ordered us to low-crawl to the bunker. The shooting had stopped. Me and the Indian kid named Buck got to the bunker first. There was an NVA soldier still alive, squirming around in his bunker, badly wounded. Without hesitation we finished him off. Buck jumped into the bunker and started taking things off the soldier's body for souvenirs. I knelt down at the edge, surveying the area, watching the choppers freely coming and going now, taking the wounded and dead away. A huge crane chopper came to take out the crashed choppers shot down earlier by what turned out to be two NVA soldiers. That's all, just two. Two soldiers who pinned down two hundred marines for three hours, shot down two choppers, killed eight men, and wounded eleven. Remarkable! Truly remarkable! It felt strange to view my enemy in this way. I thought, How glorious for them. They knew they were going to die, too. They knew it well. That was their job that day: to stop us long enough to buy time for their countrymen to regroup, resupply, dig in, and get ready for us again and then again.

"Hey, Ramirez. Look at this stuff." Buck showed me how

the soldier had laid out in a chronological order pictures of his family: father, mother, wife, children (three of them — a daughter and two sons). Instinctively I grabbed Buck's arm and told him to leave the pictures and the rest of the stuff he had taken from the soldier's body there. "Get out of the hole now!" I shouted. "You stupid fuck, get the fuck out of there before I kill you! How dare you! Leave him alone!" Buck started to go after me but stopped and said, "What the fuck's got into you?" I think he understood, but I could never check it out with him. He died the next day by our own mortar fire.

I had thought before that my life changed the most the day my grandmother died. But now I would have to say it was that day. I lost almost everything I knew and believed in. I lost my innocence, I lost my faith, I lost my own family, I lost my patriotism and national pride, and I lost what little self-respect I had left. I was stripped down to the bone. I cried that night for a long time. I cried for Roberts, I cried for those faceless men I never knew, and I cried for those gallant NVA soldiers. And I cried for me because I knew everything would be different now. I had seen life being taken, and I had taken life away.

Thoughts of an Infantryman Observing the Body of an NVA Soldier

I watched the convoy of ants,
As those coming
Crashed into those going.
It was you —
You were the terminal
For the ant convoy.
They entered you,
And left,
Each with a small bit of you.
You were lying there,
Under the sun,

Under the hill,
Under my eyes . . .
While the sun lit the jungle
Mountains and the new
Green leaves beside you,
With a warm, clear life.
There was a mangled hole,
Where the right side of
Your jaw had been.
And through the smashed
Bone and teeth,
Your life had drained out.
Now, the ants
Were carrying you away . . .
I stand here now,
With the sun,
With the hill,
With the new green leaves,
And with my life.
If we had not been here,
Would you still
See the sun,
The water,
The leaves?

— Frank A. Cross, Jr.

Five

AMBUSHED

Jensen was getting very "short" now, and it showed. He hardly went out with us on patrols and ambushes anymore. I had mixed feelings about his attitude. I understood his fear and anxiety about being so close to going home and still having to be in the bush. He had only three and a half weeks left in-country. He was scared, nervous, and happy all at the same time. On the other hand, I resented him for leaving his squad on our own with little or no guidance or leadership. Our squad consisted mostly of inexperienced marines. Half of us were people of color: two blacks, one Indian, and two Chicanos, me and another guy. I also knew that the fact that we had so many people of color in our squad had something to do with Jensen's lack of concern for us. This was the day after Roberts and the others were killed. Our own squad had taken no casualties the day before.

Our squad was being sent to the battalion CP for C rations. We had to travel about three miles. We felt relatively secure because we were walking along our own battalion line of defense. We simply followed a trail that was lined with other marines spread out about fifty meters or so apart. Each position had two or three marines.

I was walking "shadow" this day (behind the point man). Everyone was carrying a case of C rations back except me and the point man. About halfway back to our CP, we were halted by a couple of enemy shots fired in our direction from the tree line to our left flank. Between us and the tree line was an area of elephant grass about sixty to seventy meters in width. Elephant grass is commonly five to six feet tall. To our right was an open area of about fifty meters in width that dropped off into a rice paddy.

Seconds after the shots were fired, all hell broke loose. We were now being shot at by a tremendous volume of automatic rifle fire. It was as if we had walked into a prematurely sprung ambush. The first two shots alerted us in time to take some cover. If the ambushers had been able to wait another minute or so, our *whole* squad could have been wiped out by only two or three bursts of automatic rifle fire.

Our squad column was fairly well spread out just the same. The point man and I were cut off from the rest of our squad. The rest had jumped into a bomb crater we had just passed on the trail. The point man and I were unable to make it to the crater because the area between us and it was open to the view of our ambushers. Every time we made a move to the crater, we were fired on. In a sense, we were pinned down. We couldn't move or see very well because of the elephant grass. I'm sure it was hard for the ambushers to see us also, because of the grass we were now using as a sort of cover. The ambushers got frustrated and started shooting into the grass. About this time mortars started to come into our position. At first we thought they were enemy mortars, then we realized they were ours. They were coming in from far to our right or behind us, from the direction of our regimental CP. Either the marines around us had called it in incorrectly or the mortar men had made a mistake, maybe mixing up the grid coordinates of our positions and the estimated enemy positions.

The point man and I were really stuck now! If we moved

into the open areas around us, we were shot at. We were also scared to move because of the barrage of mortars falling around us. We tried to place ourselves in what amounted to mortar craters. These small indentations in the ground weren't good cover, but it was all we had. While the mortars were still coming in, almost out of nowhere two marines came flying into our position. We almost shot them. One of them was a Chicano corporal who was probably a squad leader because he started shouting orders at us as soon as he got to us. The other guy was a corpsman. They seemed to be friends. The corpsman was a big white kid, a studious, all-American type. He had short curly hair and a gentle, kind face. He was wearing wire-rimmed glasses.

The corporal was dark, small, and wiry. He looked a lot like me. He was ordering us to join him in an attempt to rush and flush out the ambushers. The corporal had a crazed look in his eyes. He was so worked up, he was spitting and drooling saliva at an unnatural rate. The corpsman's face was worried and scared. He wanted both of them to go back where they came from. But the corporal seemed out of control with his desire to get into the thick of it. For a moment I considered it, but from the look in this man's eyes, I sensed something wasn't right. I refused to go with them and advised our point man to do likewise. I told the corporal that we didn't have to take orders from him because he wasn't our squad leader and besides, we had to make it to the bomb crater where the rest of our squad was. He got very mad and called us names, something to do with our lack of masculinity and courage. Then he yelled at his corpsman buddy to follow him as he made a dive into the elephant grass. The corpsman hesitated a moment. By the look on his face, he didn't want to go with his friend. He looked at us, it seemed, for a long time, and then he said, "I understand why you don't want to go, but I have to; he's my best friend." Then away he went, following his buddy.

Our mortar rounds were still coming in on us. We decided

to get out of there by making a run for the rice paddy banks behind us, in the direction the mortars were coming from. We had to run about fifty meters across an open area to the bank. We counted to three, then ran together but spread out, zigzagging all the way. We weren't even fired at.

When we got to the rice paddy, we just jumped in. We were looking over the edge of the bank when we saw about ten meters to our left a black man pulling himself along the ground to the rice paddy. We didn't know him. We went over to where he was to see if we could help him. The mortar men had now made the right adjustment, so the rounds were being dropped into the tree line. This marine had been shot in his right thigh. He told us that he would be okay and for us to leave him there because there was a group of seriously wounded marines in a bomb crater out to the left of our position and we should help them first. He said they needed bandages very badly. The point man and I knew they were our squad.

We made a run for the crater again, without any shooting at us. When we got to the crater, there were a couple of guys who were lightly wounded but able to help the ones who were hurt more seriously. All the rest of them were seriously wounded. They had taken a direct hit in the middle of the crater. With all of them lying on the inside perimeter, it was no wonder that they all got hit. We didn't know where to start helping. The guys who were still conscious were screaming with pain and fear that they would lose their legs or arms. The ones who were unconscious were near death. Buck, the Indian kid, was near death, and there was nothing we could do.

One other kid, a Chicano from East Los Angeles, died in my arms while I was trying to stop his intestines from coming out. I don't remember his name, but I will always remember him. I can't really help seeing the image of him in my arms, struggling to live, and my attempt to push his intestines back in his abdomen as I watched the life go out of him. I can hear the sound of the corpsman's voice telling me to leave him to die because there was nothing we could do for him. Others who had a chance needed our attention. Of course it was true. Nevertheless, the feeling of helplessness I felt at that moment has haunted me ever since. The entire moment comes back to me in the form of a conscious flashback — I don't remember ever actually dreaming about this incident. I vividly reexperience it all over again when I'm awake, as if I'm there again, usually when I'm in a helpless state of mind. Not every time, but often enough that as the years have gone by I've grown to expect it. The young man's face also has become clearer to me, as perhaps the significance of his regular reappearance has become clearer to me. Although I had only once briefly interacted with him, a few days before he was killed, it was unforgettable nevertheless. He talked about his life back in the world. He showed me a picture of his girlfriend and himself sitting by a pool in his backyard. His face radiated love when he talked about the prospect of marrying this girl when he got home. He talked about the good times he and his family spent together in that pool and how that house would probably be his someday. His background seemed to be very similar to mine — that of an upwardly mobile working-class suburbanite Chicano family. However, I noticed a difference between us even then. I thought how naive and silly he sounded, going on this way about home. Didn't he realize where he was? Didn't he realize how much time he had left on his tour? Wasn't he just tormenting himself?

Only now, after reliving the experience over and over again through the years, do I realize why I continue to have flashbacks about him. He was very much like me except he was happier. His home life seemed more stable. It was an irony that seemed to repeat itself over and over again. So many of these boys who died, American and Vietnamese, seemed more deserving of living than I, whether because they seemed to appreciate life more or because they had such a passion for what they believed, they willingly gave their lives. I felt guilty that they died and I didn't because they seemed to be better or braver men.

Soon after he died in my arms, others came by to help. The shooting had stopped altogether, so we could carry the dead and wounded to a secure LZ.

By the time we finished loading everyone up, we were exhausted. We asked a captain what we should do because there were only two of us left. He said for us to go back to our CP. We started back, but it was getting dark. We had just passed the crater where our squad got hit when we saw a small group of marines standing around two bodies inside body bags. They said the bodies were found too late to be flown out. They would have to wait until morning. I looked closer at the bodies and recognized the pair of wire-rimmed glasses among the personal belongings ready to join the bodies inside the bags—those belonged to the corpsman we had briefly met earlier. I stood next to the smaller body, figuring it was the Chicano corporal, and talked to it. I said, "You stupid motherfucker, look at yourself now. You're dead, and worst of all you've taken this poor sap with you. Fuck you, you jerk! You deserve it!"

Our point man thought I was strange for saying this to a dead body and suggested we move on. It might have been strange, but there was nowhere I could put the feelings I had except into anger and nowhere to express that anger, so shouting at a corpse actually served as some kind of relief. The point man and I started out, but we didn't get much farther in the dark. We spent the night with a couple of guys who had a whole bomb crater to themselves for cover. We were being sniped at most of the night from the same tree line where the ambush had been sprung. I felt unsafe in the crater, so I separated myself from the others and went out about ten meters from the crater. None of us slept that night.

The next morning we made our way back to our CP. As we were walking in, Jensen came out to meet us. He was half smiling and laughing as he said, "So you made it through. Man, you've really had a good taste of action this last week, Ramirez. How does it feel?" He tried to put his hand on my shoulder, but I knocked it away. I yelled, "Keep your hands off me, you fucking pig! This is not funny, Jensen. If you send us out one more time without leadership and I make it back in, I'm going to kill you! You rotten son of a bitch, I swear to God, if the gooks don't get you before you go home, I will!"

I'd never seen him so scared. He went to our CO and told him I had threatened him. The CO came to me for my side of the story, and I told him what I'd said was true, and I meant it. I said I thought Jensen was endangering my life and everybody else's in the squad. I told him that Jensen should be sent home because he simply was not doing his duty, and I thought he was a racist besides. The CO agreed with me and sent Jensen home the next day, three weeks early.

After everything that had happened the day before, watching people die and narrowly escaping losing my own life several times during the day, I was primed to settle my problems with Jensen. All the anger I had felt at him all along had a chance to express itself as righteous outrage. I felt at least I could do the right thing about him.

During the next four days, we lost eleven more guys. I believe it was about the fourth day after Jensen left when we were attacked again, this time at night. That evening we were preparing for a night movement. We were very tense about it. We had been probed that evening a lot. The night movement seemed like a dumb idea to most of us. It did not make much sense to us to expect that 250 guys with full gear could move very quietly at any time, let alone late at night. As we marched along the bank of a river with the moon almost full, I kept thinking, This feels bad. Something is going to happen. I was walking shadow again, so I was at the head of the column. Our point man was not a part of our regular unit. He was a scout borrowed from the 5th Marines, who were familiar with the area. I don't remember talking to him. All I remember about him is he seemed older than most of us, very seasoned and tired looking. He kept stopping the column because he was hearing things. I cringed every time we stopped and started. The noise we were making was causing me a lot of anxiety, and walking in the sand was very tiring, mostly because our momentum kept getting halted. I remember praying to God to protect us just a few moments before the point man tripped an explosive device (a booby trap) that we were later told was one of our own GI hand grenades captured and rigged as a booby trap by the enemy. I was hit by shrapnel behind both my legs. Everyone behind me was hit. Then rifle rounds started hitting all around our position. The guy walking point seemed to be dead. I pulled myself behind his body for cover. By now the rest of the column was moving up and returning fire along with me and one other guy who was not hurt too bad. I was crying and shooting at the same time. Rounds kept hitting the body I was using for cover. After the shooting stopped, corpsmen were jumping around, checking for priorities.

I was in a panic, calling for the medic. I was afraid to touch my legs. I thought they might be mutilated. The corpsman yelled at me to shut up because I would be all right. He was right—I had caught only small pieces of shrapnel, but I couldn't walk.

We were all medevacked that night. Eight of us were wounded; one was killed. I and a black marine were the least injured. We were in the same hospital ward in Da Nang. The rest were in other parts of the hospital.

Although the circumstances of my getting wounded were horrible, at the time I could only think that I was very lucky and glad to have been hurt badly enough to get out of the bush, but not so badly that I was mutilated. My luck got better yet. As it turned out, one of these small pieces of shrapnel had severed a nerve behind my right knee, which disabled my right foot. I was unable to move my foot back and forth or spread my toes, which kept me from being able to walk. Because of this, I was transferred to a navy hospital in Yokosuka, Japan, for physical therapy.

While I was there, I met a guy who had been shot eight times. He said he was semiconscious while an NVA soldier stood over him, shooting him. It was a miracle he survived. I began to feel guilty over my "pissant" wounds, compared to this guy's.

I was in Japan for five weeks. It was winter, so snow covered the ground and mountaintops. It was beautiful, but I was unable to enjoy it. I only left the hospital once during that five weeks. Eventually I was able to walk under my own power. I was sent to Okinawa for more physical therapy, but I didn't need it. While I was there, I started experiencing sleep disturbances. I kept having nightmares about using the point man's body for cover.

The CO had recommended I see a psychiatrist. The psych doctor said it was normal for me to be upset about the incident, and it was not unusual to do such a thing. He said it might be best if I returned to Vietnam as soon as possible. He said it would be better than sitting around Okinawa, doing nothing.

I had known this was coming because I was physically fit enough for returning. I was relieved to find out that I was being reassigned also. I had been detached from my regiment, 2/26, for two months. Apparently this was too long for me to return to them. I was relieved because when I was with 2/26, we had been getting our asses kicked, and from what some guys were saying in Okinawa, this was still the case for 2/26.

Before I went on that last operation with 2/26, there had been fifty guys in our platoon. The night I and the others were wounded had reduced that number to seven. This all happened within a span of about seven to ten days!

So the minor but complicated wound had served as a blessing. I would not have to go back to such a severe combat situation because of it. My short stay with 2/26 (approximately three months) turned out to be the most intense combat experience of my combat career. I was reassigned to a new unit, 3rd Marine Division, 3rd Regiment, 3rd Battalion, or 3/3, as I will refer to it. Compared to 2/26, my time with 3/3 was a cakewalk.

Six

3/3

My drug use and abuse in Vietnam was gradual; at first I only
had survival on my mind. I knew drugs were out there, in the
villages and my comrades' packs, and I was indeed very cu-
rious about them, especially since I tried marijuana and LSD
while on my leave. I must say I actively looked for marijuana.
Although my previous experience with drugs was brief, I
thought it was just what I needed to get through the war.

I was surprised at how hard marijuana was to find at first. I
thought it would be everywhere and easy to obtain. This is
what I had been told by guys who had preceded me. However,
considering how chaotic my first three months were, if I had
found it, I doubt I could have found a place or the time to use
it. I just knew I had to have it. Alcohol had always been my
drug of choice before, but since arriving in Vietnam, I seldom
craved it. In those first few months I hardly had an opportunity to get drunk, anyway. The only place to really safely get
drunk or high was the rear areas (secured), and we were only
in the rear perhaps seven to ten days out of those first hundred
days. I don't remember that I did, either. What I remember
was being scared, worried, and lonely during those brief rests

in the rear. While in the bush, there was no room for such self-indulgences, especially since I was green. Survival and being alert were the order of the day every day.

My new situation with 3/3 was much more conducive to finding pot or, for that matter, anything else I might want. It still took a while to find out who to go to. It wasn't exactly the kind of question a marine should start asking first thing off the truck when joining a new unit. I knew marijuana was not far off now. I could smell it. Getting to know these new guys enough to find out exactly where it was was postponed because I got malaria within days of my arrival.

When I first joined 3/3, they were at the Rockpile, a fire-base, or artillery support base, that was fairly remote. My transport from there to the hospital ship *Repose* made several stops. One was in Da Nang, at a hospital at division head-quarters. While I was checking into the hospital, I was by the corpsman's desk, waiting for someone to notice me standing there in a hospital gown holding on to an IV. The corpsman was having a conversation with someone, but I felt too weak to interrupt him. I saw the ceiling spinning, and the next thing I remember, I woke up in a hospital bed in a Quonset hut, and they told me I'd been out for thirty hours in a kind of a coma. Then they apologized for ignoring me. After that I was sent on to the *Repose*. I was told I had a fever of 108 degrees when I first came onto the hospital ship. I was on the ship for twenty-one days.

I remember those first few days well because it seemed I could not sleep. My fever was so high, I was delirious. Every time I closed my eyes to try to get some sleep, cartoonlike figures kept appearing on the inside of my eyelids, like on a movie screen. The figures were superheroes from comic books I used to read as a boy. The figures were also in bright, lively colors. They kind of shot by my eyes, stiff, without arm and leg movements. Every now and then one of these superhero bodies had my disproportionately small head on their huge bodies. These visions scared me after a while. I told a nurse what was happening, and she explained that it was only the fever causing me to see things and not to worry. I supposed I was being drugged or something.

After the fever lifted, I thought I was feeling well enough to go to the mess hall on the ship under my own power, but while I was waiting in the chow line, I passed out again and was taken back to the ward. I was anxious to get off the ship because I felt claustrophobic, and I was actually anxious to get back to the bush. While I was on the *Repose,* the battle known as Hamburger Hill was going on, and I heard reports of it daily. I knew Hamburger was an army operation, but I felt that I was slacking and should be with my unit.

But once I returned, I wasted no time finding the "heads" of my new platoon. Pot smokers in Vietnam were usually called heads, as in potheads, I suppose. Most units were divided into two basic drug groups: the drinkers and the heads. Sometimes there was a very small group of "slammers," or intravenous drug users. Usually this depended on the size of a base: the larger and more secure, the more likelihood of slammers existing. I fit in right away with the heads. It helped to be from California. Anybody from California had to be cool, they assumed.

My experiences with pot to this point were very few and certainly not very cool. But I passed myself off as an old hand easily. We called marijuana "herb," which I found quite appropriate.

One could not spot a head right off in the Marine Corps because we weren't allowed to display such telltale markings as peace symbols, whether they were drawn or in the form of jewelry, at least not in my experience. The symbols were there; they were just hidden. Seeing film footage now of Vietnam GIs with peace symbols drawn on their uniforms or large shiny symbols hanging from their necks with shirts open makes me cringe. When I see it, I say to myself that those had to be army guys. Marine heads wouldn't be so loose. To be honest, I can't remember enough of the guys' names or even their nicknames. There was a group of about five of us who regularly shared herbal rituals.

A guy named Barney was one of the group I remember well. I remember how we used to make quite a ritual out of smoking herb. We used to make candles out of the wax lining from the packaging mortar rounds came in. The lining, once pulled out of its cylinderlike canister, looked like one of those fly strips people hang on their porch, semicoiled but stiff. If you simply twisted this coil until it was tight, it would make a crude but functional candle. They burned more like a torch sometimes if you didn't twist them real tight. We would have heavy philosophical conversations that I seldom remembered, but I guarantee whatever they were about, we thought it was profound. I would spend the rest of my first tour of duty with this group, doing one job of protecting firebases in several different locations. Each base had its own special problems or obstacles to getting herb. Most of these bases had villages nearby where one could find it. Sometimes getting into villages was very difficult since they were usually off-limits to us. Getting in and out of villages after curfew, especially if they were off-limits, became quite a game and adventure for me. I took on the job of provider for my group. In that first year I did get caught twice by army MPs and both times had to give them the liquor I had picked up in the "vill." Although I was truly a stoner, I got along with the drinkers well enough to help them out too.

It wasn't always like that. We had our differences in the beginning. The differences usually arose when the stoners, including myself, disagreed with the drinkers over whether at certain bases it was too dangerous at night to be stoned while on watch. However, the stoners I associated with could care less if the drinkers got so drunk they passed out, probably because the drinkers usually covered each other, as we stoners did.

During that entire first tour, I probably got drunk twice. Considering the amount of drinking I did before entering the Marine Corps, this was very odd, primarily because of the ready availability of alcohol. In a sense it was a substance sanctioned by the military. It was usually everywhere, even in the most remote of places because, at least in my experience, the Marine Corps actually provided it in a rationed quantity. Of course it was never anything more than beer. Any other kind of booze had to be bought. When we got beer rationed to us in the bush, it usually was two beers, and we also received two sodas as well. Guys who didn't drink or want their beers would trade them for sodas. I normally traded my beers for sodas, as did any good head. I didn't start drinking again until I was out of Vietnam.

I was able to indulge in this drug use because my time with 3/3 was much less intense than my time with 2/26. I was assigned to a 106 platoon. The number 106 stands for antitank weapons that look like small artillery pieces but are not considered artillery because they are recoilless, direct-fire weapons. Artillery is an indirect-fire weapon that recoils. Since we rarely used these weapons offensively (because the NVA had few tanks), we primarily used them for defense on firebase perimeters. We moved around a lot, spending anywhere from a week to a month at a particular base. Occasionally we were used in infantry combat situations. Doing firebase protection, although relatively safe, was frustrating, especially the times we spent at C-2, a firebase at the demilitarized zone (DMZ), so close that we could actually see the enemy's flag with binoculars and sometimes an enemy soldier waving at us just before they sent rockets soaring into our base.

We spent most of our time keeping up the maintenance of our 106s in case we had to use them. We never did. Besides the possibility of being overrun, our worst fears came from the constant rocket and mortar attacks we suffered. The rocket attacks were almost daily occurrences. Hearing the rockets come in was terrifying. They sounded like speeding locomotives descending on you from the sky. Our platoon's weaponry limitations prohibited us from retaliating.

One day Barney and I were walking from the mess hall at C-2 in broad daylight, and we could hear the rockets coming. We looked at each other, then just ran. The bunkers we lived in were heavily fortified, with several layers of sandbags piled on top, so that they could withstand direct hits. We headed for our bunker to get out of the open. I had outrun Barney, actually passed the bunker, and was hiding behind the sandbag bunker surrounding our gun. Barney had stopped outside the sandbag bunker and hit the dirt when the first rocket hit. I looked up, and out of the dust I saw Barney flying through the air after a second rocket hit. I saw him land almost on his feet, jump up, then continue to run. He dove into the bunker. When the incoming stopped, I ran into the bunker to check on Barney, and he hollered, "I got a Purple Heart! I got a Purple Heart!"

"You idiot," I said, "you could have been killed." He'd actually gotten hurt worse in the fall down the stairs to the bunker, dislocating his shoulder, than by the shrapnel. I'd been hit by shrapnel from the first explosion too and not even noticed it. I had a concussion and small fragmentation wounds to my head, hands, and arms, but this time I did not need to be hospitalized.

I still had not made any real friends, probably because I avoided it as I had sworn to do after Roberts's death. I worked at keeping to myself. Most everyone in our platoon, a group of three squads, knew something about what I had been through with my previous unit, so I was allowed to be antisocial if that's what I wanted. Our platoon tended to be spread out over two or three different firebases, so we rarely saw members of the other squads. A squad in 106's platoon consisted of one gun; a squad leader, who directs fire; a gunner; an A-gunner (assistant gunner, who loads rounds for the gunner); and two ammo men. Usually we only carried one ammo man. I was an A-gunner, then later a gunner.

So I really didn't get involved with guys in this unit, who didn't seem interested in getting to know me, either. In fact, when I first reported to the unit, the staff sergeant in charge of the platoon would barely make eye contact with me, let alone shake my hand. What little eye contact he made was with both disdain and indifference. It was disturbing to me at first, but it was the nature of our work that we hardly saw him, anyway, so the fact that he treated me as if I did not exist was just as well. As a result I had no expectations about advancement, whether in rank or leadership. Eventually I did become a team leader of a 106 gun, but not until the last month of my tour. Being treated like I was invisible had its advantages, like the time army MPs picked me up for being in a village after curfew. When they caught me, I had a sack full of booze. As they patted me down the MP felt the bundles of ten-packs in my fatigue leg pockets. He looked up at me and grinned devilishly but said nothing about the herb he had just found in my pockets. Instead he told me, "We're going to take this booze so that when we take you back to your CO, we don't have to tell him we found any contraband on you, OK? Do you understand?"

"Oh yes," I said, "I understand," and I thanked them.

This was neither the first nor the last time I would be caught in this same predicament with nearly the same results. I was very lucky. When these MPs escorted me back to my CO's tent, my platoon sergeant and my CO were so drunk, they both kind of squinted at me and the MPs. One of them spoke up, I don't remember who, and asked, "You're in our platoon?" I said "Yes," and thought, Oh, boy, these guys are really fucked up. They told the MPs they would take care of it and that they could leave. After the MPs left, they looked at me, then at each other as if looking for an answer about what to do with me. The officer merely said, "Get out of my face and stay out of the vills." I said, "Yes, sir," and that was it.

Near the end of my first tour with 3/3 our 106 platoon was used in a special battalion-size operation as a regular infantry platoon. Up to this one operation we had been used strictly as protection for various firebases. Our division was responsible for the area from Dong Ha to the DMZ. Although my 3/3 combat experience was mild compared to my time with 2/26, this particular operation we participated in was rather intense and somewhat bizarre, if not outright surrealistic.

The preparations for the operation started days before we went out. Several of my comrades in our platoon were very excited about being in a major battle. We knew few details, but we knew it was something big, bigger than anything these men had experienced before. I had already gone through several such combat operations in a very short time, and I had no romantic notions about what might happen. I was scared and worried about how my comrades would react when the shit hit the fan. It disturbed me that they seemed to think this was some kind of big game or adventure. Not one of these thirty-five or so men had any real infantry combat experience, even the ones who were now short-timers, with less than three months left on their tours. The short-timers' lack of fear was particularly weird. Several of them looked at this operation as a last chance to get some real action before they went home.

In a way I understood it. It was frustrating not to be able to retaliate for the rocket attacks. So for some guys this operation was a chance to take revenge.

Knowing I was the only guy in my platoon with real combat infantry experience, my platoon leader assigned me the M-79 grenade launcher but gave me no other responsibilities, like team leader or squad leader. This oversight was typical of how I had been handled since joining 3/3.

We were treated unusually well as we prepared for the

operation. We were outfitted with new fatigues and boots and given steak dinners with all the proper trimmings at least twice before we went out. They also provided us with all the beer and soda we could drink the whole time we were in the rear. It was party time before the day of reckoning. Because I had experienced this before and knew what it really meant, it was hard for me to get into the party spirit. For me all it meant was this might be my last supper or some other sap's last supper.

Somewhat to our surprise, we were ordered to saddle up that night. We were going to be deployed by truck convoy. By the next morning we were ready to move out, with only a few minor details yet to be taken care of, like in my case, rounds for my M-79. I had been concerned about this since my superiors had replaced my M-16 and ammunition with the M-79 only, no rounds, no sidearm, nothing, just the weapon itself. They kept telling me not to worry, that I would be given the needed ordnance before we were deployed. Now that we were getting ready to move out that night, I was very nervous about not having any ammo or any other weapon like a pistol, rifle, and so on. All I had were a few hand grenades. I was frantically looking for ammo or someone to get me some. It was not a simple matter of walking up to an ammo tent or something; one had to have authorization or a requisition. When I did find someone who could help, an ammo sergeant, he just stared at me like I was the problem, almost as if to say, "What do you need ammo for? You're just carrying the M-79. . . . " I felt like I was having a bad dream. Once we were loaded onto the trucks, there was complete silence. The convoy of trucks moved up Highway 9 slowly and silently, with parking lights on only. As before, I found these night movements of such a large force and our attempts to do it quietly humorous at best and at worst critically stupid.

Our destination was an area called Leatherneck Square, somewhere at the extreme edge of the territory of the Northern I Corps. The convoy stopped just past a village, letting off an entire company, then continued up the road perhaps a mile or less, close enough that we could still see the vill on the horizon. This time the rest of our battalion, two and a half companies, got off the trucks. We started moving out in a column parallel to the vill toward the foothills. We might have been marching for fifteen to twenty minutes when the village became illuminated by gunfire. We all went down.

We assumed the company we left off near the village, Hotel Company, was engaging the enemy. We also expected to help or to be fighting soon ourselves.

I was near panic. I still did not have any ammo. Again I was put off and told not to worry. I was practically begging for at least one round from somewhere! Surely there was someone else carrying an M-79 in this company. I asked my CO. Again he just looked at me as if I were making a big deal out of nothing and told me to take it easy, that we were not going to be involved in the battle going on in the village, anyway. As it turned out, neither was Hotel Company. The battle was being fought by elements of the Army of the Republic of Vietnam (ARVN), the South Vietnamese army, and the local militia against a regular North Vietnamese army unit, the size of which was not immediately known to us. We watched and heard the battle rage on into the night. All of us were growing more anxious about what we were going to do or were supposed to be doing there.

We kept moving most of the night in the same direction toward the foothills. We stopped just before dawn and sort of slept. Shortly after dawn we moved out again. Eventually we set up and dug in a perimeter position somewhere between the village and the foothills.

Our commanders had sent out observation posts (OPs) outside our perimeter. The idea was to get an early account of the NVA soldiers who had attacked the vill the previous night, before they reached our position on their way back to the hills. It was a perfect setup. All we had to do was wait. The NVA unit walked right into the trap. The hole I was in with two other guys was very close to our CP. Watching our commanding officer of the battalion, a full bird colonel, kneeling on one knee talking on the field radio, reminded me of General Custer's last stand. However, the outcome would be quite different. We overheard the guys out on the OPs reporting that they had spotted NVA soldiers cautiously approaching their positions. The colonel was asking them how many they could count. They would report back, giving different amounts each time and asking if they could retreat to our position each time. Each time the colonel would say, "Request denied. Hold your position. I want an accurate count."

We started looking at each other, wondering out loud when he was going to let them come in. We could sense the fear in their voices. Finally they called in, saying, "We think we've been spotted, and we're moving back," without waiting for approval. That was the last we heard from them. The colonel had been using the information about the numbers and positions of the enemy to call in air strikes on them. The airpower had caught an entire company of NVA, crack infantry in wide-open terrain. By the time what was left of this company reached our position, they were running into our perimeter with their arms in the air, surrendering. Some of our guys were shooting them regardless. It was literally a slaughter. I was still without ammo or an effective weapon.

Our platoon commander came to our position and ordered us to split up and spread out. I exploded in anger. "What the fuck am I going to do with no ammo, bluff them? Fuck you!"

His reaction was, "Oh yeah, that's right, you have no weapon. Sorry about that. Here's my .45. Keep your eyes open. See ya." With that he ran to the other side of the perimeter to join the killing frenzy that was going on.

I could hardly believe what was happening. Guys were running around whooping and howling like this was some kind of rodeo or something. I stayed where I was told to. I was more scared that I was going to be killed by our guys, the way everyone was acting. I spotted the foliage moving out in front of my position. I thought, This is great — someone will probably come out with an automatic weapon, and I'm sitting here with a popgun. I yelled, *"Dung lai, dung lai."* I think that meant give up, or surrender. Whatever it meant, two very young men came out, holding their arms in the air. They looked like teenagers. They were shivering with fear. Some of my comrades spotted them and ran over to us, and right off they started abusing the prisoners. I threw up my arms and said, "Why don't you just kill them?" One of the guys said, "Relax, we're just having some fun." They took them away. Those boys did not appear to be crack troops to me.

The body count for the day was forty-two NVA dead and thirteen captured, many of whom were wounded. We lost four guys and had no wounded.

That night our squad pulled one of the ambush assignments. An ambush assignment is nothing more than going out after dusk, setting up in a strategic position, then lying in wait for the enemy to come by. My squad leader was very nervous about it because it was something neither he nor anyone else in our squad had done before except for me. He asked me to help him. I said, "Sure, if you think you could get me a rifle and some ammo, I'll take over the ambush as soon as we leave the perimeter." The ambush was routine and uneventful. I spent most of the night awake, unable to get the sound of those guys' voices on the radio out of my head. I was also very concerned that what I had witnessed that day was a mass murder rather than a battle. Later we learned our own General Custer won a Silver Star for his performance in the entire operation.

While I was with 3/3, I had other experiences that were not combat intensive but still had an extremely powerful effect on me.

During one of our regimental troop relief movements I

had the incredible good fortune of crossing paths with my good friend from boot camp training, Paul Graff. Seeing him again was both remarkable and dramatic, considering the circumstances.

Our unit, 3/3, was being deployed to relieve another battalion in our regiment, 3/2, who held a small firebase near the Laotian border. It was a typical firebase gouged out of the wilderness: a hill or mountaintop had been flattened and defoliated with explosives, and heavy equipment with barbed wire had been strewn around the perimeter. As our chopper was descending onto this eyesore in the middle of nowhere, I could see marines waiting to the side of the LZ to board the same chopper we were coming in on. We were their relief. As we got closer to the ground I could make out some of the faces waiting. When I recognized Paul Graff, I could hardly believe it. I was both excited and sad. I knew we had only a second to talk because chopper pilots don't like to linger.

As we filed out and Paul and his group were filing in, we stopped just long enough to exchange our exact unit assignments and agree to find each other if we got lucky enough to end up working the same operation or in the 3rd Marines Division rear area. There was a good chance of that, so I hoped I might be able to see him.

Seeing Paul was a huge flashback to the "world." He was an unlikely surprise connection, and I was looking forward to talking with him again. He did get a chance to mention he had been in-country just three months, which made him approximately four months behind our original training group. It had been seven months since I last saw him, being taken away by ambulance with his leg broken at Camp Pendleton, just days before we were both supposed to leave for Vietnam.

He was upbeat and cocky as usual. Other than on that day he broke his leg, Paul's attitude never seemed to change, whether he was experiencing the rigors of boot camp or stood as now on this hilltop in the middle of a war zone. I felt lucky to have seen him. I was anxious to talk to him about everything that had happened so far, to hear about his ordeal, and, of course, simply to reminisce about home.

It would be about a month before I got back to the 3rd Marines rear area. The headquarters for Paul's unit was not far from ours. When I first asked the desk sergeant about Paul, he said, "We don't have anybody by that name in Fox Company." Then he stopped his thought process, looked up from his paperwork, and said, "Were you good friends?"

Immediately I got this terrible feeling. I said, "Yes, why? What's wrong? Say it!"

The desk sergeant said, "He was killed two weeks ago."

The image of Paul and me talking at the induction center in Oakland flashed through my consciousness first. Then several other mental pictures passed through. Like him looking back at me with that cocky grin as he crossed the goal line after burning me for a ninety-two-yard touchdown, and the time he was coaching third base in front of our dugout, mouthing off to us and us giving it back to him.

Then came the image of his dead body. I wished I couldn't picture it so easily, but it was a picture I had seen many times. It also occurred to me that it was wrong that Paul died instead of me. It was one of the mysterious ways in which the Lord moved. After all, I felt that Paul was the better man of the two of us who had walked through the induction center door about a year before.

One other thing I felt that day struck me as weird at the time. A sense of relief and calm came over me because the odds that I was going to make it home alive were better now since Paul had been killed. I felt guilty for thinking it and guilty for surviving.

In November 1969 the entire 3rd Marine Division was being withdrawn. Almost everyone with less than seven months remaining on their tour of duty was getting out of the country early: they were either being reassigned to Okinawa or sent home. All others were being reassigned to units remaining in Vietnam. In my case, it made little difference because my tour of duty was almost up, anyway—I had only one month left out of thirteen.

Almost all the guys I was with in 3/3 were able to take advantage of this troop withdrawal. In fact, we all traveled together by way of ship convoy to Okinawa. The trip took four days.

We arrived in Okinawa about two weeks before I would be heading home on leave. I was lucky in a sense because first I had two weeks to party. My rotation date was December 18, but something happened to my records. They had been misplaced, I was told. While I was in Okinawa this time, I worked very hard at numbing myself with drugs and alcohol. It got to the point where I didn't look forward to going home. I had met a Korean girl who was a dancer at one of the many bars available to servicemen near Camp Hansen (a marine base on "Okie"), and like many a serviceman who has passed through this place, I thought I was in love and wanted to stay there, maybe to go into the restaurant business or farm with her and her family. It was as if I didn't want to ever face anyone I had known before, not even my family. I knew opposition to the war had been going on at home, but I didn't want to see it.

I don't remember that I ever found any herb while in Okinawa, but I did find and use LSD. I probably would have taken just about anything I found except heroin. I had seen a few use it while in-country, but it didn't appeal to me. Although I had tried smoking opium and liked it, I still had no interest in the "rush" guys talked about. The idea of sticking needles into my body myself was out of the question. My drugs of choice remained alcohol and marijuana with an occasional hallucinogenic here and there. I was really very reckless and out of control. My memories of those weeks are like looking through a kaleidoscope.

Walking or riding down narrow, neon-lit streets and alleys that seemed to tunnel endlessly, every other storefront a bar or brothel, I was constantly late for muster. Sometimes I arrived to formation just as my name was being called, still in civilian clothes and high.

At least three nights that I can remember I was escorted back to base by MPs for seemingly being lost. And indeed I was lost, in an altered state of consciousness. On one of these nights I found myself sitting on someone's grave, leaning back against a gravestone with two MPs kneeling in front of me, asking me if I was all right. I remember looking out to the ocean behind them, wondering if Mike boats, small troop carriers, had landed on those beaches during World War II. The MPs kept asking me questions: "Who are you? What are you doing here? How did you get here?" I could only tell them who I was and what base I was from. They seemed bewildered that I was so far from my base (forty miles or so) and that I didn't know how I had gotten here. We could only speculate that I had taken a cab. I only had a few dollars, which was not enough to take a cab back to my base. Apparently I was deep into the country, far from any town or village. I was in a small graveyard that looked out to sea. The MPs said they had been called by a farmer whose house was nearby. The farmer had said he was awakened by me hollering into the night. They said the farmer was scared.

There was, however, one man who I had somewhat of a relationship with that developed near the end of my time with 3/3. Our relationship became important at this time because he helped with the problem of my records being lost and also my problem of not wanting to go home.

Chuck was my last squad leader while I was with 3/3. He might best be described as a "good old boy." He was from a small town in Georgia called White Plains. Chuck was college educated but at the same time a very down-to-earth older man (twenty-five years old). We had our differences, mostly about racial issues, but generally we got along. There was one dialogue in particular I remember that perhaps describes what kind of relationship we had. He called me J.R., my initials.

"Chuck, I'm getting tired of you calling Billings a nigger all the time. He has a name, you know."

"Why are you bothered, anyway, J.R.? You're white, you know, not black."

"What are you talking about, Chuck? Are you blind? I'm not white, I'm brown, you idiot! Where I come from, I'm considered nonwhite; you know, a spic, greaser, dirty Mex, wetback. Get it?"

"Boy, oh, boy! Doesn't take much to set you off. Look, J.R., I don't care about all that hogwash. All I know is that I ain't never seen a Mexican before I went to college, and even then it was in a book. Besides, we beat the hell out of y'all in a war, anyway. Right? Fair's fair, ha, ha. Come on now, it's over, J.R., right?"

"Fuck, I don't believe you, Chuck. That's like me saying you should stop calling Billings a nigger because after all, y'all lost the Civil War!"

"That's enough, J.R. You're not making sense. I'm going to settle this right now! Billings! Billings! Hey, Billings! Come over here. I want you to tell this boy something."

"What is it, straw boss?"

"J.R. says I ought not to be calling you nigger. What do you say?"

"Can't say it bothers me one way or another, cracker! Ha, ha!"

"See what I mean, J.R.? Old Billings lives not more than twenty miles from my place, and we get along just fine."

"This is a waste of time. I'm sorry I brought it up."

"Yeah, I suspect you are, J.R. I suspect you are." Chuck spit on the ground as usual.

While we were in Okinawa, Chuck was trying to talk me

out of this fantasy I had about staying there, and at the same time he was trying to find out where my records and orders were so he could help me get home before Christmas.

"J.R., I have to tell you, buddy, I think you're a little crazy with all this talk about staying here in Okie. Why don't you introduce me to this girl and her family so we can see what you're getting yourself into?"

"Look, Chuck, you're not my squad leader anymore. I'm the same rank as you are now, so don't play that father-advice shit with me!"

"Suit yourself, J.R., but it would be a hell of a thing for your family to spend another Christmas without you."

"I don't care about them. I stopped writing months ago, anyway. For all I know, they're out protesting or some shit like that!"

"Man, you got a real problem. You know, you could call them from here. It wouldn't cost you anything. Why don't we try, okay?"

"Oh, why not! I'm running out of money, anyway. Maybe they can send me some of the money I've been sending home."

Overseas phone call, limited to three minutes, sponsored by the Red Cross:

"Hi, Mom. Thought you'd never hear from me again, huh?"

"Son, that's a terrible thing to say! We've been worried about you. You haven't written in three months. The Red Cross said you were okay but that they couldn't make you write if you didn't want to."

"Yeah, they came out and scolded me. At any rate, I've only got a few minutes on the phone, so what's up? Is the old man still staying drunk?" .

"Son, please don't talk about your father that way. He's fine. Why are you being so mean? What have we done? And when are you coming home?"

"I'm not sure. My orders got screwed up. Mom, I have to

go. I'm sorry if I hurt you. I'll call you when I find out. I'll work on getting home before Christmas, okay?"

"Son, please be careful. We miss you very much."

"Okay, okay. Good-bye, Mom!"

Chuck said, "Now that wasn't bad, was it?"

"Oh, fuck off! Stop treating me like you're my father."

"Now we need to find out what happened to your orders, okay?"

"Sure, sure. What the hell. After all, I'm still in the Marine Corps for two and a half more years. I don't suppose I can get away with staying here in Okie, anyway."

Chuck said, "Now you're talking!"

My initial feelings when I found out I was going to make it home by Christmas Day were still ambivalent. On the one hand, I was happy I had survived and was going home, but on the other, I wasn't sure what I was going home to, and it wasn't possible to feel proud of what I had been doing in Vietnam. The result was I simply felt numb most of the time.

It was a strange feeling, after this very long and eventful year, to be actually going home and not be all that crazy about it. What I mean is that while I was in Vietnam, I was anxious to go home like most guys, but now that it was really happening and I was relatively safe from combat and I had survived, I was not looking forward to going home any longer. I was really very frightened at the thought of it.

While I was waiting in Okinawa to go home, it never occurred to me that I would return to Vietnam in five months at my own request.

Seven

CHRISTMAS, 1969

I arrived in Ontario, California, at El Toro Marine Air Base late on Christmas Eve night. I was off the plane and off the base in no more than twenty minutes after I checked in with some guy at a desk.

"Here's your orders for twenty days of leave; here's a voucher; here's your orders for your next duty station. Don't be late back from leave, have a good time, and good luck, Marine."

The voucher was for a loan I'd arranged because I didn't have any pay coming. I couldn't cash the voucher until I got to Moffett Field, the nearest base to home. I didn't have any cash, but I didn't care. I was just glad to be home. I stood out in front of the base with my seabag next to me, and a cab pulled up. I told the guy I was broke and could he tell me where Western Union was.

"You just get back from Vietnam?"

I said yeah.

"And you don't have any money?"

"All I've got is a voucher I can't cash here."

"Man, that's not right. I'll give you a ride to Western Union, and you can pay me when your money comes in."

So he took me to Western Union, and I wired my parents. I looked out once, and he was there, waiting. It took a while for the money to come, and when it did, I went out to pay him. He was gone. I took the bus to Los Angeles International Airport, then got on a plane for San Francisco.

Waiting for my plane in Los Angeles, I called my parents to tell them when I was going to arrive. Some stewardesses were talking nearby. I could hear them, but they didn't realize it. They were talking about their respective passengers. "All I've had is businessmen and baby killers," one woman said to the group. They all giggled. I suppose it was a joke, but it hurt me deeply just the same.

On the plane to San Francisco, I kept thinking about what the stewardess had said and wondered what my family thought of me. Did they think I was a baby killer, too? I started getting scared all over again, like right after a firefight.

While I was walking through the terminal, I thought about splitting in some other direction, but then I saw them. My parents didn't recognize me at first, so I was able to just look at them for thirty seconds or so. My mother looked sad and scared. My father was so drunk, he could barely stand up. Now I really felt like going in another direction. It was clear that in the year and a half that I'd been gone, my father's alcoholism had gotten much worse. He hadn't been able to come to my graduation from boot camp, and now he couldn't even come to pick me up at the airport sober. It was depressing.

I didn't spend much time around the house. I spent most of my time partying. After being home for only a couple of days, I decided that twenty days of leave after what I had experienced would not be fair or adequate. I tried to get an extension of my leave through the proper channels, but my request was denied. So I took the matter into my own hands. After my twenty days expired, I just didn't go back. My father didn't approve, but my mother thought the same way I did. What were they going to do to me? They couldn't possibly do anything worse than what I'd already been through.

On the twentieth day of my unauthorized leave, or UA, from the Marine Corps, I was driving a friend's car — a black, beat-up Volkswagen that was itself a moving violation. I was on my way to a date that I hoped would be better than my two other attempts at dating since being back in the "world." I got the distinct impression that both of those girls were doing a favor for my friend who had set us up. I really thought this date would be different. I had known this girl before I went into the military. She seemed to have an interest in me then, so why not now? I had almost forgotten about the Marine Corps.

I had about an hour before the date, so I decided to drive around and practice not being nervous and awkward, wondering if I should talk about Vietnam to this girl or not. I noticed a cop had been following me for a couple of blocks, but I wasn't worried. After about a mile he closed in on me, then pulled me over.

Now I was scared. I had no driver's license and had been UA for twenty days. Without a driver's license or a California ID, I might be arrested and my military status would be found out. Maybe if I copped to being a marine on leave, he might give me a break and let me go on my way. I was wrong.

He said he stopped me because my license plate light was out and I had bald tires. While he was checking out the car for other violations, he ran a check on my name. They found a warrant for my arrest on a traffic ticket from the last time I was home on leave. I knew my mother had paid that with money I had sent home. I wasn't worried and told the cop there must be a mistake.

The cop laughed and said, "Tough!" He arrested me and had my friend's car towed. While we were riding to the jail, he mentioned that because I didn't have any military orders for leave in my possession, he would have to call the MPs for clearance in their jurisdiction before I could be bailed out. Now I was very scared.

My mother found the receipt for the fine, but I was still being detained because I had no orders to prove that I was on legitimate leave. The MPs were on their way to take me into their custody. I tried lying about the orders, saying that my mother would bring them along with the receipt for the fine payment, but it didn't work.

While I was being booked at the jailhouse in Palo Alto, the deputy sheriff who was booking me seemed to take a special glee in harassing me. He kept trying to stare through me with his cold, blue, piercing eyes. But my eyes wouldn't let his in. He was older than me, maybe twenty-five to twenty-eight years old, but he behaved more like an eighteen-year-old. I was halfway through my twentieth year. He finally became frustrated with not being able to stare me into anger. He started jerking my arm around as he was fingerprinting me, making racial insults, and laughing. Still I just stared at him. The insults were not new to me, so they didn't hurt as much anymore. Then he said, "So you just got back from Vietnam, huh?" I didn't answer. "What did you do, burn shit for a year? I hear the Mexes were used to burn shit."

"No, I didn't burn shit. I killed people. I was a grunt."

"Your hands are too soft. You couldn't have been a grunt."

"It doesn't take much effort to pull a trigger," I said.

That shut him up, but now I was in a rage I couldn't express for obvious reasons. Motherfucker! Calling me names was one thing, but to demean my sacrifice was quite another thing altogether.

The MPs finally came and took me to the brig at Treasure Island, near San Francisco. After I spent a couple of days there, they put me on a plane to my next duty station, Camp Le Jeune, North Carolina. Camp Le Jeune, also known as "Camp Le Goon," had a population of about forty thousand marines and their dependents. The nearest town, Jacksonville, had about twenty-five thousand people. The next city of any note was Charleston, about fifty to seventy miles away.

Camp Le Jeune was a bummer for me. Because of the twenty-one extra days I personally extended my leave, I was facing a summary court martial as soon as I arrived. A summary court martial is the lesser of the three types of military judicial court martial. The next level is called a special court martial, then the highest level is called a general court martial. A summary court martial is conducted solely by a captain or an officer of higher rank, usually by the defendant's own commanding officer. The process is usually brief. The presiding officer has complete authority. The defendant has no right to counsel, and UAs are usually cut-and-dried.

My sentence was reduction of rank from E-4 to E-1 (corporal to private), a fine of one month's pay ($360), and a suspension of my right to apply for transfer to any other duty station for a period of one year except for duty stations such as Guantánamo Bay Naval Station in Cuba, a Mediterranean flotation brigade, or any base in the western Pacific, which really meant Vietnam. To say that Camp Le Jeune was miserable for me is putting it lightly.

I did meet up with a guy who had been in my last unit in Vietnam. But about a month after we were at Le Jeune, he found out he was going home. He had enlisted for three years, but because of his military occupational specialty (MOS), 0300 (0300 is the designation for any MOS that is infantry related: 0300 Rifleman, 0361 Machine Gunner, 0351 Antitank), he was being released fourteen months early. The Marine Corps was letting 0300s out early because they had more than they could use for stateside garrison duty. My friend's MOS, 0351, was the same as mine, but because I had signed up for four years, I still had two and a half years left and was ineligible for the fourteen-month early release.

Now I was really fried at that recruiter. Not only did my

length of enlistment have nothing to do with my VA benefits as he had told me, but having signed up for four years was interfering with my discharge when the Marine Corps, by its own admission, had no practical or constructive use for me any longer.

My friend tried to help me before he left. He said he had a good rapport with our new platoon commander at Le Jeune and that he would talk to him for me. The new platoon CO and I hit it off very well. He seemed to understand me a lot more than I was understanding myself at the time. A lot of his understanding, I now believe, came from his own combat experiences.

He was a first lieutenant but had not started out his career in the military as an officer. From what my friend told me, he had been an enlisted man as recently as two years earlier. He had spent a tour of duty in Vietnam as a combatant, then returned again, that time as an officer. Apparently he had earned his officer's commission in between his two tours of duty in Vietnam. At any rate, he had considerable experience as a combatant and as a leader of combat units.

He tried to help me get some of my lost rank back as fast as he could, giving me jobs within the platoon that carried a lot of responsibility. With the added responsibilities I had to have some of my rank back to substantiate my authority. These moves were not received very well by the rest of the members of the platoon, especially by the marines who had yet to experience Vietnam. They began to resent me. They didn't respect or care about what I had gone through in Vietnam. In fact, no one ever tried to find out about my experiences there. I don't think it helped much when our CO let me try out for our regimental baseball team.

These weren't bad problems to be having, considering the status I started out with when I arrived at Le Jeune. I had earned one of my lost ranks, back up to E-2, PFC (private first class). I had a pleasant enough job. I got to travel with the baseball team, and most important, I had the support of my immediate CO.

But it wasn't enough. I hated the place. And I hated the Marine Corps. I felt like a prisoner. I hated everything about the region, which I remember most as acres and acres of dead and dying trees. The people who lived there seemed to be slowly and painfully dying, too. The only thing to look forward to every day was cleaning your weapon and picking up trash. One of the things that disturbed me the most at Le Jeune was the atmosphere — it seemed a race war was about to erupt between the blacks and whites.

On garrison duty, we didn't have a common enemy to fight against, so blacks and whites fought against each other, and blacks and Latinos fought against each other. Once I got in a fight with a group of black marines who were playing a game of craps in the barracks. I told them it was after hours and they should knock it off. It turned into a fight. There was one black guy who asked me, "Who are you with? When the shit goes down, whose side are you on?" He pulled out a .22 rifle and said, "We're all packing here." And it was true — they had private, unauthorized guns.

I felt isolated, not wanting to choose sides and not wanting to fight with both the blacks and the whites. There were some Puerto Ricans at Le Jeune, but there weren't that many Mexicans, and that didn't feel very good, either.

I was not adjusting to life as a garrison marine. The prospect of having to spend another eight months there had become unbearable. I started to grow increasingly withdrawn and isolated. I'd buy some pot and go out in the woods and get stoned. Or go out and get drunk. One night I got so drunk in the woods that I got lost and didn't get back on time for muster. I always hung out by myself, went to town by myself. I wouldn't talk unless it was absolutely necessary and even then only the minimum. I began getting into fights almost daily. I started fights when I was drunk, and usually with really big guys. Then I started going out into the woods, practicing to set up ambushes for those who fought with me or laughed at me. I wanted to kill them. People were laughing at me because of my behavior. They thought I was a kook.

Looking back now, I can see that I was in much worse shape than I realized. I was desperate and in despair, my drinking was out of control, and I probably wanted to die. There was no term for it at the time, but now I know I was already suffering from post-traumatic stress (PTS) syndrome.

I decided to get out about four months after I got there. Because my choices were limited to Guantánamo, Cuba; a Mediterranean float (on ship most of the time); and the western Pacific, my prospects for relief were not that good.

From what I was told, Guantánamo was much like being in prison. I thought I could adapt to the hostility but not to the inability to leave the base. The Mediterranean float was often facetiously referred to as a "Mediterranean cruise." From what returnees told me, the "cruise" was really a kind of constant floating patrol waiting for something to happen in the Mediterranean region, with infrequent stops at various ports for R and R. There were also stops for practicing maneuvers in a hostile Greece. Life on a ship for a prolonged period of time can produce a great deal of tension, especially when sailors and marines are concerned. This option was also not unlike being in prison.

I chose to go back to Vietnam. My rationale went something like this: If I go back, maybe I'll get lucky and be assigned to noncombat status, maybe I'll be cut some slack because I've already spent a year in combat, or maybe I won't have to finish the whole tour of duty because of troop withdrawals. Plus I knew that life. I mean, I knew how to survive in it. It was a simpler life, in a sense. Everything was provided for me: food, clothing; I didn't even have to wash or shave while in the bush if I didn't want to. I didn't have to talk to anyone if

I didn't want to. As long as I was doing my job, I could withdraw into my own world without having to explain it.

Life in the bush is cut-and-dried. When you wake up in the morning, you pat yourself on the back, sip your coffee, and say, "Well, I made it another day and night without getting killed," and that's that. There were times in the bush when I felt a powerful sense of serenity in the middle of insanity. A kind of peace in the simplicity of knowing that I could die at any moment and that I was powerless to do anything about it. I actually missed the excitement and enchantment of the countryside and the people who lived there, regardless of the horrendous war going on.

Compared to what was going on inside my head and heart, going back to Vietnam didn't seem at the time like such a bad thing. Of course now I do see it as a bad thing. Even though I felt the war was wrong, I could not stop it or change it. And my sense of duty to my fallen comrades was strong. At that time I didn't have a coherent political analysis of what was wrong with the war, which would have allowed me to take a principled stance against it. Yes, it was horrifying, but I also knew it would go on with me or without me. If I was there, at least I could affect what was going on around me. And without really knowing it, I think I was going back expecting to die, subconsciously believing that my death would represent a sort of justice.

My CO tried to talk me out of it, promising me more rank. He said that he understood what was happening to me and insisted that I would be sorry once I got back there. He said he thought I wanted to be dead and that I was romanticizing the war. I disagreed and said that as bad as it was for me there, it was never as bad as here. He said he'd pray for me; I said I'd appreciate it more if he sent some good coffee every now and then.

I was out of there by the end of the week, on my way home for twenty days' leave and then back over to Vietnam.

Eight

SECOND TOUR

I arrived at Da Nang Airfield on June 27, 1970, one day before my twenty-first birthday. I was assigned to Company B, 1st Battalion, 7th Marine Regiment, 1st Marine Division, or, as I will refer to it, 1/7. 1/7 was an infantry unit. So here I was again, sitting in a foxhole on my birthday, wondering, What have I done? What have I gotten myself into? I knew I was taking a chance that this might happen, being back in a foxhole, but still I was in a state of shock. In fact, those first few days back in Vietnam are the source of a recurring dream. I find myself sitting in the jungle again, shaking my head, thinking, You're not going to make it this time—the odds are against you! Maybe this is what you want after all? To die here? Maybe I thought it was what I deserved for being a part of that injustice.

Our role in Vietnam had been dramatically changing for about a year. The bureaucrats, politicians, and military had a name for it, the "Vietnamization" of the war. I had *always* operated on the assumption that the Vietnamese were doing most of the fighting.

I spent my first month with 1/7 isolated and detached from

the rest of my platoon as much as possible. I had a lot more combat experience than anyone else in my squad or platoon. But my rank, E–2, made me just another rifleman or fire team leader at best. (A fire team is about half a squad, four or five guys.) Keeping to myself was easy. I was left alone as long as I did my job.

We usually operated as a platoon (forty to fifty men, three rifle squads, and one special weapons squad) in a designated area of operation (AO). We shared our AO with the other two platoons of our company. We hardly ever pulled together as a company. In fact, we spent more time working with platoon-size elements of the ARVN than we spent with elements of our own company.

My new squad leader was a big redheaded, middle-to-upper-class, white jock-type kid, a real gung ho marine. He was always chasing people he couldn't see, like snipers or rustling bushes. I couldn't help but laugh at him, and neither could the ARVN soldiers. He also like burning things. One time we came across an old woman way out into a "free-fire zone," or hostile area, where nobody was supposed to be except NVA or Vietcong. Our orders were to arrest such people and destroy their property. Man! He was salivating at the prospect of being able to burn this old woman's hootch. I argued with him about the likelihood of this woman really being a VC. I asked if it didn't seem more likely that the reason she was still here was because she was too old to make the move. He wouldn't listen. He had his "orders," and he had his lust to burn that hootch. He burned the hootch and arrested the woman and turned her over to the ARVNs that were nearby.

But usually our duties with 1/7 were much more routine than anything else I had experienced. Every third day our squad had the daily patrol of our AO, and every third night we had night ambush duty. This duty was not combat intensive. Most of the combat was focused on the ARVNs, to whom we were now regularly attached. For instance, one day while on patrol with the ARVNs we were all resting near a village well. Most of our group was dangerously bunched up to one side of the well, but the ARVNs were safely dispersed around the entire area. I was a safe distance from the cluster of marines, leaning up against my pack, watching. Two ARVN officers in tiger-stripe fatigues walked up to the well for water, then momentarily paused to talk. Suddenly a burst of automatic rifle fire cut them down right before my eyes. Everybody took cover, but the shooting had stopped. No marines were hit. My squad leader wanted to chase the attackers, but the squad didn't like the idea. Our guys realized that the burst of fire would have produced more results if it had been aimed at them.

It was clear to me that the VC's priorities were to single out the ARVN forces, at times completely avoiding us if they could. The evidence grew with incidents like this just about every day. I can now see that the VC were trying to nip the "Vietnamization" of the war in the bud.

Much to our squad's surprise, our gung ho squad leader took advantage of an opportunity to go home early. I don't know the details, but I think his mother had influence with a congressman or someone like that. He was one of the first middle-class guys I'd seen in Vietnam, and when those guys started being part of the war, stuff like what happened with this squad leader became common. A lot of middle-class families found ways to get their boys back. The rest of us didn't have those kinds of connections.

Our new squad leader was inept but kind. He only lasted two weeks. He also went home early, but I don't remember the reason. Our squad was now without a leader. We were also without a ranking competent prospect. Our platoon commander, First Lieutenant Capps, asked me if I would take over the squad. No, I said. I didn't want to be responsible for anyone except myself; moreover, it would be difficult to command the needed respect without the rank.

He said being part of a combat unit made me responsible for others whether I liked it or not. He said he would get the appropriate rank for me as soon as possible, adding that the guys in the squad already respected my judgment, so the rank really didn't mean anything to them or to him. I still said no. Then he said that if I didn't accept the position, he would give it to a man I disliked and distrusted very much. I said yes.

My priorities changed rather suddenly, but really very smoothly and painlessly. It was as if the new responsibility was a kind of "rush" in itself. It was the kind of excitement and exhilaration I had only briefly experienced before, but somehow this time, unlike my previous opportunities for leadership, I had complete confidence I could do the job. Of course I was scared at the same time, but fear can be a positive force if kept in perspective. Some fear is healthy and critical to a soldier's survival. I took my job and responsibility for others' lives very seriously. Rarely have I felt so alive and important. Perhaps never is more accurate than rarely. I was so proud to have been recognized as a leader and to have my experience valued.

This development brought on some positive changes for me. First, I was transformed from a loner into a leader, then I made my only true friend while in Vietnam, Lieutenant Capps.

Lieutenant Capps was from northern California. He stood about five-foot six, very short for a marine officer. Because of this, his nickname was Peanuts. He had a boyish face with an almost permanent mischievous expression on it. He also had a high-pitched, squeaky voice that made you want to laugh whenever he tried to yell.

Up to the day he made me a squad leader, I didn't know much about him except that like the rest of the platoon, he was inexperienced in combat. But Peanuts learned fast, mostly due to his admission that although he was in command, he was open to learning from those of us who had more experience. He often asked the squad leaders for their opinions when faced with difficult decisions, whether about our relationships with the Vietnamese or combat maneuvers and strategies.

Now that I was a squad leader, I could try out my ideas on how at least to behave well in this war, especially now that we knew most of our efforts were for nothing. When I first took charge, I pointed out to my squad that we had been going for long periods without making contact with the VC or NVA. When we did make contact, had they noticed the hostility was usually directed at the ARVNs we were now constantly with? I also showed them the correlation between our conduct in the villages and our contact with the enemy. For example, if some members of a squad decided to steal some food or a hammock, or abuse the children, or rape or try to rape the women in one of the hamlets they passed through, the next marine patrol to go through that area would get sniped at or ambushed. We would stop chasing everything that moved, we would keep a low profile while on patrol, and we would not steal, hit, or step out of line in any way. Also, if there was a need to take chances, we would delegate the risk to the ARVN soldiers. In a sense, we would simply go through the motions of our assigned duties except when attacked.

I wanted to make sure that my squad acted this way because it was the right thing to do, but I didn't put it in those words. I just convinced most of them that this defensive attitude would save lives. Why take chances when there were so many rumors of units being pulled out?

One guy in particular didn't like *any* of *my* ideas. He resented my authority and said he didn't see why our activities in villages should be restricted. I really didn't believe he was mean, but he was immature and full of testosterone, and I think he was frustrated. He felt like we had a right to take whatever we wanted in the villages because we were "helping these people." He also thought that the "pretty girls" should not be off-limits. What he meant was that he wanted to be able to buy them, but I think given the right circumstances he was capable of rape. I only remember him as Calloway. He can best be described as an "urban redneck." He disliked blacks, so I assumed he also disliked Chicanos.

There was enough tension between us that I thought I would have to fight him, but I didn't want to. However, if I was going to command respect in a combat situation, I didn't want to have to worry about him or, more important, the others. So instead of fighting Calloway, I gave him a leadership position. Then I won him over almost completely when my prediction about "extracurricular activities" in villages came true.

Our squad was resting on the outskirts of a village one day when a boy about ten years old came running up in a panic. I knew the boy from having come through the area a couple of weeks before. He was crying and yelling at the same time, speaking half in English and half in Vietnamese. He grabbed my hand, trying to lead me into the village, gesturing for me to follow him. Calloway was with me; we had been going over our maps. He followed us.

The boy led us to a hootch full of commotion. A group of children had surrounded two marines from our platoon. The kids were punching and kicking them, trying to pull them away from a young girl. Both of these guys were recent additions to our platoon. One was our new corpsman and the other was our new platoon sergeant, second in command to Peanuts. Both were also inexperienced in the bush. They had been with us maybe a week. The corpsman's inexperience was not that unusual, but the sergeant's was. Up to that point in his Marine Corps career, he had been a supply man. He was a staff sergeant (E–6) who, in his words, "wanted to experience combat before the war ended." He volunteered for the duty and the Marine Corps obliged him, much to our misfortune. I hollered for them to stop, and they told me I could have "some," too, if I wanted. Calloway thought this was funny. I told them if they didn't stop, I would tell Peanuts. They grudgingly let go of the girl, and she and the other children ran away. One child, about seven or eight years old, stopped to spit at the sergeant's and the corpsman's feet. The sergeant lunged and slapped him two or three times before I could grab him.

"Who do you think you are, Lance Corporal?" the sergeant said. "Let go of me, or I'll have you written up."

"You do that and I'll make things very difficult for you out here, Sarge."

"Are you threatening me, Marine?"

"If we get hit tonight or tomorrow," I said, "it will be both of your faults, and if anybody from my squad gets hurt because of it, you both can consider yourselves threatened by me personally."

With that, they both went off huffing and puffing about my lack of regard for their rank. But they knew they were wrong.

I told the other squad leaders to be extra careful that night and the next. We hadn't experienced any kind of contact with the VC or NVA for more than three weeks, but I felt we were vulnerable now.

That night our squad and one other set up with plenty of open area around our nighttime defensive positions. As usual, our command post was set up in the middle of our small perimeter. The CP is usually occupied by the platoon commander (Peanuts), the platoon sergeant, a corpsman, and a radioman. There were three of us in our hole on watch that night. Three men were in each of the other two holes of our squad, positioned on each side of us. It was about 9:00 p.m. when I decided to get some sleep. I was lying flat on my back with one eye and one ear still open as usual. I was semi-conscious, wondering if anything would happen, when I heard faint pattering, like bare feet running. It seemed to get louder and closer. The next instant I heard two thuds on both sides of our hole. I instinctively covered my head and turned over.

The grenade explosions shook the ground, lifting my body up and then dropping it. My ears were ringing. I looked at the kid who had been sleeping next to me, and he seemed to be okay. Then I crawled over to the next hole to see how the kid on watch was. He was crouched down, holding his head, with blood coming from his ears. He was suffering from a concussion but had no other wounds. We had escaped without serious injury. After a moment Peanuts and the sergeant came diving into the hole. I was firing back with a grenade launcher, lobbing rounds in a scattered pattern into the night. It was really pretty hopeless, but it seemed the only thing to do. "You're a good squad leader, Ramirez," Peanuts said after watching me return fire.

I looked at the sergeant and at the corpsman, who was now attending to my wounded man. "You stupid motherfuckers!" I said. "You're responsible for this! Peanuts, these two jerks caused this to happen by harassing a village girl earlier today — I'd bet my life on it! If you don't do something about it, we will!" The sergeant and corpsman were embarrassed. They both apologized, but I saw no real remorse from the sergeant, who kept reminding me who was in charge. The corpsman was visibly shaken. For the remainder of our time together, the medic became more serious and professional. But more important, he became more humane toward the Vietnamese.

There was another important result — Calloway now understood why we should not step out of line. Our life in the bush for the next month was characterized by mutual respect. We still didn't like each other, but we at least agreed on the most important issue at hand — how to survive this mess.

I think Peanuts and I got along because we were both Californians. We spoke the same language. We also found out we had one other thing in common. I had used marijuana twice before going overseas, then about seven months into my first tour of duty, while with 3/3. I had used it whenever it was safe to, at a firebase or in a rear area. Now I was quite familiar with it, but I didn't have anyone to share this secret vice with in 1/7. There's a widespread belief that everybody in Vietnam was on drugs, and it's true that there were a lot of drugs in rear areas. However, I never witnessed excessive drug use while I was in the bush. It wasn't possible to get away with. It wasn't tolerated by my peers, and I didn't tolerate it, at least in what I perceived as a dangerous situation. I can't ever remember drugs being a factor of poor morale, at least not in the bush. If any drug was used, it was only pot.

One night while at the 1/7 rear area, I had sneaked away from our platoon group, which had been drinking most of the night, to smoke a joint in private. I was relishing the joint because I had made a conscious choice not to drink alcohol while I was in-country this time. Pot was my only vice so far. I thought I had slipped away unnoticed, but Peanuts had been watching all of us from a hidden vantage point.

I saw him walking toward me and quickly extinguished the joint, flicking it away as if it were a cigarette. His first words were, "You don't smoke, do you?"

"Sometimes when I'm in the rear, I get nervous about the drinking, so I smoke."

"No need to waste a perfectly good smoke because of me," he said, and reached down to pick up the joint. "Funny cigarette. Is it Vietnamese?"

"Yes." Now I was noticeably nervous. I thought I was going to get busted and thrown into the brig. But with his best mischievous smile, Peanuts pulled out a joint of his own and said, "I like Vietnamese cigarettes, too. Try one of mine."

I couldn't believe it! From then on we had our own private little secret. We usually talked about California, the war, and the war at home. We shared many beliefs, especially about behaving well and treating civilians humanely.

But not everyone in our company shared our beliefs. I began to have difficulty with members of the other platoons of our company. In particular, a couple of Chicano squad leaders and an Indian kid who was a fire team leader from another platoon took my bush attitude as cowardly and confronted me with it once while we were in the rear.

This was one of those days in the rear when it was more like one of the company picnics my dad used to drag us to. We had been provided with as much beer as we could drink. Everybody was drunk, these three guys especially. They started in on me because I wasn't drinking. Then they asked what it was I thought I was doing, disgracing our heritage in the Marine Corps by "pussyfooting" around with the Vietnamese. Didn't I realize that *everyone* was the enemy? I said I didn't think they understood the difference, so it was a waste of time to explain. They boasted about how many kills they had and how many wounds they incurred getting them and reiterated I was a disgrace to the race. I tried walking away, but they kept after me, calling me names, trying to provoke me. The Indian kid persisted, challenging me to a fight. I was tempted because he was so drunk he could hardly stand up, but I thought better of it, figuring I would have to fight them all if I picked on the most vulnerable. Nothing much else happened, but the incident hurt me deeply because it came from my *carnales,* my own kind. It also served to confuse me more than I already was. Was I cowardly in choosing this position? Was I a disgrace to my race?

I started once again to have serious problems. One day on patrol, after weeks of no contact with the enemy, our point man stopped our column and called me up. When I got there, he was crouched down and very nervous. His eyes were wide as they could be. He said he thought he saw a person sneaking down on the other side of a rice paddy dike, just out to our flank. We both watched for a while, then I saw a person bob up and scurry along the dike a few more feet. It looked like the person was armed because a long, narrow object seemed to be slung across his back. We waited quietly. The figure bobbed and scurried another few feet. This time I yelled for him to come out from behind the dike. He did not. I sighted in with my rifle and waited for him to move again. We had called in as soon as we suspected it was the enemy. Our CP was now squawking over the radio, asking what was going on, but we didn't reply. We were intent on the person behind the dike. When he bobbed again, I had him dead in my sights. In a split second I could see that the person I was about to shoot was an old woman with a bundle tied to a stick. I was squeezing the trigger, and I think I could have stopped, but I didn't. Although I realized the woman probably was unarmed, I fired, anyway. In that instant I felt that I had to do it, I had to release the tension. And I was afraid to hesitate — a part of me knew that to hesitate was to get killed. That fear silenced the realization that I wasn't aiming at a combatant.

Half of the squad was already circling around behind the dike as I had ordered. The CP heard the shots and became more frantic over the radio. I told the radioman to tell Peanuts we were okay and that I'd explain the shots when we got back in. I went down to see what I'd done. I had wounded the old woman very badly and probably would have killed her if it hadn't been for all the stuff she was carrying. Cooking utensils and small pots and pans saved her life, absorbing most of the impact of the round. The corpsman became angry that I hadn't called in a medevac chopper. I so shocked myself that I couldn't perform my duties; Calloway called it in. The woman was evacuated. I assume she lived.

When we got back to the CP, Peanuts was very pissed off that we hadn't communicated more of what was going on. He demanded an explanation. I told the whole story, and the squad verified it. However, I didn't tell anybody that a split second before I shot her, I realized the woman was a noncombatant. Everyone else thought it had been a legitimate accident, and that's how Peanuts wrote it up.

The truth is, I probably couldn't have stopped myself from pulling the trigger, but I've always believed I could have, a belief that reflects my guilt more than the truth. God, has the face of that woman haunted my dreams! This incident is also the source of another recurring nightmare. In my dream I'm being pursued by Vietnamese, the military, and American civilians. They run me to exhaustion, and when I fall to the ground, they all start kicking me, chanting in unison for me to repent my sins and account to those I hurt.

At the time I tried to explain the shooting away to myself. It had been a long time since we had made contact with the enemy, and tension was building. Something had to give. If it wasn't going to be me, it would have been someone else. I often thought the periods when nothing happened were the worst because we were waiting for the inevitable. Once it did happen, we would be too involved in the fight to be scared. Once it was over, we were glad it had happened. Much of the fear is in the *waiting* and the *wanting*. If you're scared by the waiting, a part of you must *want* it to end.

Shortly after this incident, we got word that we were being withdrawn as a unit. It didn't mean much, though. Most of our platoon was reassigned rather than sent home. I was disappointed because Peanuts hadn't had enough time to get me all the rank he promised. I would like to believe that if my leadership opportunity had been played out, my preoccupation with marijuana and other drugs would have dissipated through the rest of my combat career. As it turned out, I had the misfortune of simply being reassigned to a new unit, 1/2, 2nd Battalion, 1st Regiment, 1st Marine Division. My remaining time in the Marine Corps would take a downward turn. Suddenly my opportunity for advancement and, more important, my chance to further prove I had the ability to lead, ended. I had been given the job of a fire team leader, in charge of about half a squad with my new unit, but the entire situation was so different. I didn't adjust in a constructive way. The morale of 1/2 was very poor largely because we were on night shift.

Our platoon operated from a permanent perimeter position that included our own seventy-five-foot observation tower. Our regiment formed an outside perimeter around the entire city of Da Nang. On rocket belt duty, we were approximately within rocket range of the city. The inside perimeter had the usual barbed wire strands that were laid out in rows one-eighth mile wide, leaving a space from the outside of the city to the inside of the wire. Outside that perimeter we formed the rocket belt perimeter, a defensive position that was without barbed wire or fences. Our positions were about eight hundred to one thousand meters apart, each position having its own smaller platoon-size perimeter with an observation tower in the middle of it. The platoon positions resembled small permanent base camps.

We ran four-man night patrols all night long. We called them killer teams. Sometimes we had only three guys on a team. Our goal was to patrol the area constantly at night in order to ward off rocket attacks. Our patrols usually took about an hour or more. During the day we slept, rested, cleaned our weapons, took drugs, and drank. We seldom left our own perimeter. The Vietnamese would usually bring whatever we wanted to buy up to our "wire": sodas, beer, liquor, herb, opium, heroin, and speed in the form of a French over-the-counter product named Obesitol. The fact that it was monsoon season didn't help morale, either. Our job was to keep moving and, very important, to navigate through our patrol accurately because there were other patrols in the area. The constant rain made our conditions extremely difficult and at times impossible. Frankly, we were probably more likely to hurt each other than to get hurt by the VC or NVA.

Although we weren't technically in a secured rear area, the atmosphere was the same as if we were. I had learned to dislike and fear life in the rear areas. The rear was the place I'm sure all those surrealistic notions about the war came from. It was all there. Drugs, the black market, prostitution, gambling, racism, and violence. The rocket belt duty was the first time I saw intravenous drugs used on a daily basis or in a direct combat situation. It was also the first time I saw marines in command look the other way at such behavior.

This assignment posed many more dangers for me than the bush. I felt threatened mostly by the drug abuse and racial violence. In this case, the racial tensions were black versus white. The closer one got to the rear, the more intense the tension was. At some point one had to choose a side. It was difficult to remain outside of it all.

My first impressions about all my new comrades was that they were flakes. Accidents waiting to happen. Very careless and loose. It was as if they weren't in a war zone. I tried to keep to myself, but I was lonely and depressed before I arrived. Isolating myself wasn't really what I wanted. The more involved I became with the little drug cult that existed, the less I gave a damn.

Our hootches were nothing more than holes dug in the ground with a few sandbags around the edges. We made roofs by wedging our plastic ponchos between the sandbags. These hootches were some of the worst living conditions I experienced — sleeping in the open bush with no shelter was far more preferable. Our holes were hard to keep dry or warm. We often found ourselves sharing them with rats, snakes, and large insects. At times, sharing them with each other was obnoxious. It was easy to get on each other's nerves. It was no wonder we spent so much of our time getting high on whatever we could find. I can see us now, uncomfortably huddled around a candle, wet, sniffling, looking at each other, not really talking, waiting to go on patrol. Not able to escape outside because it was steadily raining. Quietly passing around a bottle of Obesitol or booze, trying to achieve some comfort. Very few of us really got along with each other.

The black guys seemed to be the tightest group. They congregated at one of the bigger, better hootches. They had spent some extra effort building it. You could almost stand up in it. Whites were not welcome. Working together wasn't a problem for blacks and whites, but outside of that, there was segregation and conflict. People would simply go off to their separate groups after patrols, not ever talking again until it was time to go back out. Because I was not really white, I was allowed to enter the exclusive world of the black marines. Being able to slide back and forth from the white world to the black world fairly easily was somewhat of a paradox because I found it easier than trying to settle in with my own ethnic group. The other Chicano marines thought I was too assimilated.

Being allowed into the black marines' world was not easy, though. Invariably someone would have a problem with my presence. Even when I was personally escorted by a black marine, someone would snicker, grunt, or yell out their disapproval. I usually befriended at least one or two black guys, because if I didn't already have herb, I could find it easily through them or for them. I also was very generous with it; being willing to share my herb and connections usually helped with any social interaction. "Brothers," a term used by most black men in Vietnam, would typically spend their spare time together gambling, playing cards and dice, singing harmony, and smoking herb. The use of herb, or any other drug for that matter, wasn't necessarily any more of a preoccupation for the black marine than it was for any other specific group. Frankly, in my experience, most everybody used some kind of self-medication when in relative safety.

My time with 1/2, which lasted maybe two months, was the lowest point of my combat career, clearly the point where I gave up trying to be a good marine. I stopped caring about most everything. My attitude changed for the worst either because of the work we were doing or because our group had a morale problem that led to the drug abuse. The drug abuse, in turn, had a bad influence on me. While I was there, I started doing Obesitol, which had a much more powerful effect on me than anything I'd used before. The name seems to have implied it was intended as a dietetic aide. It came in approximately six-or eight-ounce amber-colored glass bottles. We paid one or two dollars for a bottle. I took quite a liking to Obesitol. It wasn't the first time I had used an upper. My mother had introduced me to them in the form of diet pills when I was a teenager. She had offered them to me for some discomfort I was having. "Try these, they'll make you feel good." Eventually I felt better, but I enjoyed them so much I continued to use them whether I was feeling good or bad. I had discovered her stash in a large jar hidden away. My use turned into abuse very quickly, but my mother's access to these pills, which weren't prescribed to her, suddenly ended, and so did my experience with them. As fond of them as I had been, I did not try to find another source.

Although I had used pot, it was child's play compared to this. As my abuse increased, I stopped paying attention. Out on patrol I became more and more careless. It got to the point where I just didn't care about anybody or myself. I lived for the end of my patrol, when I could get to my little hootch, get high, and then nod off until it was time to take my team out again.

It may be that what I perceived to be a very big problem, drug abuse, with this unit was indeed only my problem. However, I did feel that my life was in greater danger because of the amount of drugs and alcohol consumed all the time, not just during off-hours.

As with most stimulants, the down side from Obesitol was extremely depressive. During one of my bad days, a day when I was crashing hard, a brother we called Bookie because he always had a book in his hand suggested I try some smack, or heroin, to smooth things out. I was surprised because I didn't know Bookie was into smack. I knew there was a small group of slammers around, but I wasn't sure exactly who they were.

Bookie was about five-foot nine, thin, and wore glasses. He moved between the black microcommunity and everyone else easily. Most everybody liked him. He introduced me to a few other guys that he shot up with. In my memories they are shadowed, silent, faceless men. I was scared, but I was ready. I had smoked opium before and enjoyed the dreamy, euphoric high, but it also frightened me because I didn't feel grounded. I felt like I was free-floating, unable to control my body. Shooting smack, I was told, was far more of a rush. I had watched guys do it before, partly fascinated and partly scared. I had often wanted to try it but was scared I'd like it too much. Besides, the idea of sticking needles into myself gave me the creeps. The image of turning into a withered-up junkie had kept me from following through. But Bookie was not my nor anyone else's stereotype of a junkie. None of those guys who Bookie shot up with looked the part. I was ready. This Obesitol was kicking my ass pretty hard. Just this once, I thought. Just to get through this crash.

Bookie suggested I try "skin copping" it, which involves sticking the needle in a sensitive area of skin. Sometimes I'd see guys kind of pinch or raise an area of skin to stick the needle into. The idea was to experience it superficially, without injecting it directly into a vein. It seemed less wicked somehow, so I agreed.

I was surprised by the sensation — it was much more physical than I expected. When the rush came, I felt scared at first, but I rode with it and tried not to resist it. Soon I did feel better. I was relieved that I didn't pass out. The rush settled into a tingling sensation all over my body. I was in what would be best described as a euphoric state. I could easily have fallen asleep.

About this time the monsoons got very heavy. It had been raining on and off (mostly on) for days, but not like this. It started raining very hard while my fire team was out on patrol. We couldn't see each other even though we couldn't have been more than two arm's lengths apart. We could hear radio traffic between other units and ours about the heavy rains. Patrols were calling in complaining that they could barely walk. Some were requesting to get back to base camp because they couldn't see. We were pretty worried ourselves, but from what we were hearing on the radio, no one was being allowed to return to base, so we figured it was a waste of time to ask. We decided to find a piece of high ground and sit there, pretending to be on patrol. We had checkpoints to call in when we reached a certain quadrant of our planned patrol. We would estimate about how long it would take to get from point *A* to point *B* and then check in as if we were there. This tactic actually had a name, sandbagging. I usually didn't approve of it, but this was a dangerous situation. We were having a hard time keeping our bearings. We were afraid of running into another patrol, and we also had a pretty good idea of where we were at that point, so we didn't want to risk getting lost.

After we made it back to base camp, we had about three hours before daybreak. The rain seemed to get worse. Over our field radios we could hear other patrols having problems walking and navigating. The irrigation ditch within fifty feet of our position was now a raging river, its banks quickly claiming more and more ground. We quickly gathered and packed our gear and moved from one piece of high ground to the next, just ahead of the water. By dawn only two pieces of high ground were left, a large knoll near the center of our perimeter, where the brothers' main hole once was, and our seventy-five-foot observation tower, which also had our command post situated at the base of it. Most of the platoon was now in the tower or standing under it, holding on to its legs. About five or six of us were left out on what guys now were calling Brothers' Island. The water raged between us and the tower. It was impossible to cross without the use of a rope between our positions.

Our entire battalion was experiencing the same problems. The night before, our platoon sergeant had tried to convince our battalion commander to go on standby alert in order to evacuate our platoon in case we got flooded out. He told them about the small creek that was getting bigger by the hour. They told him they were aware of the possible danger but not to worry. Our platoon sergeant also requested that we cease our patrol activities — we were in much greater danger of killing each other than getting rocketed on a night like this. "Request denied. Continue your patrols. Out."

"Request denied. Hold on. Request denied. Hold your position." God, I hated those words. Hearing them likely meant someone would die. They usually made some kind of promise like, "Help is on the way. Our advance reports are that you are in no danger." Like many times before, they were wrong. I was one of those guys still out on Brothers' Island, and I can tell you that crossing that river was one of the most frightening experiences I have ever had. Several times as I crossed, I almost lost my grip on the rope. I could still walk on the bottom, but if I didn't make sure that each step was somewhat anchored, the force of the water could have easily swept my legs from under me.

Our biggest challenge was the last guy, because there was no one left to make sure the rope didn't come loose from the saturated ground. Fortunately everyone crossed safely. But while we were waiting to be evacuated, we heard report after report over our field radios of other units who were still missing men at dawn.

By the time choppers came to evacuate us, there was no ground to stand on. We were hanging from the tower's framework. The choppers hoisted us two at a time out of the top of the tower, pulling us up on a double-pronged hook that resembled an anchor. We were ordered to drop our packs so we could fit through the small opening under the bottom of the hovering choppers. For obvious reasons, we were only allowed to take our ordnance: our ammo and weaponry. They promised our personal gear would be picked up later. It was going to be picked up, all right, and we all knew it wasn't going to be by our guys. The nearby villagers were in boats, laughing at us all hanging from the tower's legs. Of course, now I see how funny we must have looked. They were patiently waiting for us to leave so they could get our stuff.

The "stuff" meant a lot to us. Any connections to the real world we had were in those packs. In my case it was several rolls of film, a camera, a transistor radio, letters, writing material, photographs, and other personal mementos. One in particular was the prayer felt of the Virgin Mary my great-grandmother Angelita had blessed me with before I left for Vietnam. With all the commotion, I had forgotten that several days before I had transferred all my important personal belongings from my person to my pack. I didn't want it to get wet. It was customary to secure our belongings in several layers of plastic bags in our packs, especially during the monsoon season.

When I realized what had happened, we were at some base. I have no idea where it was. It just seemed to be the closest island in this sea of water we were flying over. It was an awesome sight. I had never witnessed a flood before, let alone flown over one. Seeing only treetops poking out of the water, people casually floating everywhere in their boats, was an incredible experience for me. When we finally got to a base, we were told we would wait there until the waters receded.

I don't know how many days we were there, maybe a week or so, but it seemed it was only ever nighttime. We were told that only one man out of our entire company was lost in the floods. We did not believe it. It had to be more; we heard the radio reports of missing men. It made us angry because we felt it didn't have to happen. They shouldn't have forced us to continue our patrols in such conditions and should have helped us when we first requested it.

My spirits were low. So were everyone else's. We went from one hellhole to another, but in this one we didn't even have the few items that gave us some comfort. No home. No stuff. Our only relief was drugs and alcohol. I don't remember that I ever found any herb there. I doubt it would have mattered. I do remember this, although I try to forget it: I wanted to commit suicide here.

While on watch one night, after several days of drinking Obesitol and beer, I thought I would end it all. I had had enough. I sat in my hole with a grenade in my hand, pin pulled and thrown away. I thought when my hand got tired, I would simply let the grenade fall into the hole with me. The guy who came to relieve me thought I was joking. I warned him not to get in the hole, but he did, anyway. After a short time he asked me where the pin to the grenade was. I had thrown it outside the wire. His eyes grew large and serious. He climbed out of the hole and asked how long I had been holding the spoon of the grenade. I didn't know, maybe an hour or more. He yelled out for the duty commander. Pretty soon our platoon sergeant came, and he initially reacted the same way my relief had. It didn't take him long to realize I was having a problem. Someone else came, an officer. I had never seen him before. He was a part of our larger company unit. What I remember about him the most was his voice.

He sat himself down on the edge of my hole with his legs hanging down inside. I moved into a corner and sat on the ground, holding the grenade with two hands, which were getting tired. Someone handed this guy a pin. He told everybody to leave. I told him not to try anything because I would sit on the grenade if he got any closer. I had been holding it for about two hours now. His voice was very calm and serene. He asked me if I was a religious man. "Yes," I answered.

"You know," he said, "it's a sin to take your own life. It would be a shame for you to end your life this way, after what you have been through, and then not go to heaven." He asked about my family. I was crying now. He said, "I'm going to pray for you now. Will you pray with me for your family? They will be very hurt by your death." We prayed out loud together. The sun was coming up now, and I was relieved by the warmth. The sound of my own voice praying was warm, too. I started to ask God for the strength to carry on. Just like when I was a kid. It had been a while since I last prayed. I thought, God must be angry with me for not praying more often.

"Why don't we put this pin in the grenade," the officer said, holding it up for me to see. "You must be getting tired of holding it." I was. I told him I would do it, but he would have to get his legs out of the hole as my hands were very shaky. He threw the pin at my feet, then got out of the hole. I put the pin back in.

At first my platoon sergeant was angry at me. "We could and should arrest you," he said. "You are government property, you know."

The officer who had helped me said, "If you promise to see the chaplain today, we will not charge you with any offense." Of course I agreed. The chaplain's aide told me to come to mass the next morning.

It was a relief to go to mass. I had forgotten what a powerful experience a good mass could be. The chaplain's words were just what I needed to hear. After the mass, I asked the chaplain for a private talk about my problems. I told him everything, including a very critical assessment of the combat readiness of my platoon. I told him I feared for my life because of it. I primarily blamed the abuse of drugs and alcohol and our working conditions. He originally promised not to tell my commanding officer. I told him I wanted out of the Marine Corps or at least out of Vietnam. As a result, they arranged R and R for me, which I would get to take soon, and I was told I probably just needed a rest. Later, I was surprised to find out that my chaplain had told my commanding officer everything and that when I returned from R and R, my commanding officer and I would discuss my problems and requests further.

After a few more days at the base we'd been evacuated to, we returned to our platoon base and tower. The Marine Corps never did pick up our personal belongings. Our stuff was strewn everywhere. It appeared that the nearby villagers had gone through everything, leaving only letters and pictures. To most of us these were really the most important items. It was muddy, but the remnants of our belongings sat dry, on top of the mud, as if they had been scattered just before we got there. I found my stuff in a general area. After finding several pictures, letters, and my Bible, I figured I was lucky. But just as I was going to give up, I saw something sticking out of the mud. It was my prayer felt of the Virgin Mary that I had laminated some time before.

The sight of it glimmering in the sun gave me such a sense of warmth and peace that I knew everything would be all right, somehow. It was like a small personal miracle. Indeed, it was a sign for me. My prayers had been answered. My felt, or should I say my faith, had been restored. It was more than finding a simple memento. It was the sign I prayed to the Lord for. I realized just then why I had been carrying it. I had forgotten the solace, peace, and serenity I derived from prayer and faith in my own holy spirit. I decided from then on I would trust that voice in me.

It didn't work out that way, though. I was to lose my faith again.

I decided to take the R and R in Australia to think about what to do next. While I was waiting for my flight, an announcement came over the PA system saying that there was still room on an R and R flight to Hawaii leaving in twenty minutes. My flight was not leaving for another hour and a half. Both R and R ports, Hawaii and Australia, were seven days. Earlier I had overheard a guy say he was going to Hawaii, then getting on a plane to California to have at least a couple of days at home before returning to Hawaii for his flight back to Vietnam. This sounded very tempting to me, but I only had a few minutes to decide. I had about two thousand dollars on me, some of it back pay and some I got by exchanging currency on the black market. I decided to go home.

In Hawaii, I bought a return ticket, took a cab to a men's store for civilian clothes, then took the same cab right back to the airport for a flight to Los Angeles and then on to San Francisco. I don't think I was in Hawaii for more than an hour.

I don't know who was more surprised when I got home, me or my family. My mother was now working for an alternative medical clinic in Redwood City called The People's Medical Clinic. The clinic was right in the middle of a barrio. My father had really hit the skids with his drinking problem. My family had gone from a split-level home on a corner lot to a run-down apartment in the barrio, all since I left for the war.

My mother's new job had changed her thinking about the war, and now, after hearing about my most recent problems, she convinced me not to go back, at least not for the moment. She told some of her coworkers and friends about me, and they offered to help.

First, they referred me to The Law Commune in Palo Alto, then they got a psychiatrist to see me and to document a case for a medical discharge. This was a very hazy period for me. I remember most of it as if I were being led around like I was a zombie. I had completely put myself in my mother's and her friends' hands.

I had been led to believe by The Law Commune that it was possible for me to get out of the Marine Corps with a medical discharge, based on the fact that I had become dependent on drugs as a result of trauma I had suffered. The Marine Corps had been sending my mother notices that I was AWOL in Australia and that they were looking for me. Obviously they had no idea where I really was. Five months passed, and I had seen three different psychiatrists from Stanford Hospital through The People's Medical Clinic. All the doctors at the clinic were Stanford alumni, as were most of the lawyers at The Law Commune. My case had also been handled by three different lawyers.

At some point I had managed to get a job at the University of Santa Clara as a prep cook. I spent a lot of time partying. But after a few months I was ready to go back and face whatever it was that I had to face. It was hanging over me. I had to go back, one way or another, and face the consequences.

My mother's friends got together what they thought would be a "good" case. My lawyer's name was Ron Romines. Ron called the nearest marine base at Treasure Island and arranged a meeting and my surrender to the CO there. The conditions of my surrender were that I not be jailed until I had a medical evaluation by the military to confirm or dispute the psychiatric evaluations done by civilian psychiatrists. The civilian doctors recommended that I be given a medical discharge because I had become a drug addict as a result of having to participate in an unjust war. They said I had become a psychological casualty. I was trying to destroy myself with drugs. They pointed out that I had no experience with drugs prior to the military.

The CO at Treasure Island was a colonel, a "full bird," and he was tough. He didn't like any of this business, but he had given his word to Ron, so he grudgingly listened. Then he said I was to be taken to Oakland Naval Hospital immediately after our meeting for one week of psychiatric evaluation, after which time a decision would be made by *him,* based on the navy's evaluation of my drug disability and combat fatigue.

Well, instead of one week I was confined to a locked ward for three. I wasn't all that surprised, but by the second week I was acting out violently because I was pissed off about being placed in a ward full of psychos. I was not psychotic. The more I made a fuss, the worse it got. I was given a lot of tests that first week and kept on drugs for the next two weeks. They said if I didn't take Thorazine and Stelazine, I would have to stay indefinitely. So I cooperated. I don't remember a whole lot about what went on during those two weeks except for one guy in particular who was supposed to have killed several of his friends who had cheated him during a crap game in Vietnam. I don't remember his name, but he was a huge black man, maybe six-five or bigger, weighing in at about 220 or 230. Everyone was scared of him. He went around the ward threatening to kill people, then he'd come back begging forgiveness and offering little pieces of paper as gifts. I shared a room with him and two other guys. Sometimes he'd wake up and start talking to us as if we were all back in the jungle together. He would get mad if we didn't play along with him, so somebody always talked to him.

After the three weeks, Ron and I went before the CO again for his final judgment. He said that the navy psychiatrists had found me to have a passive-aggressive, neurotic disorder and that they recommended I be administratively discharged, which meant he could grant me an administrative discharge that was either under honorable conditions or other than honorable conditions—it was solely up to him. Also in the navy's evaluation was a statement that read something like this: "John is quite capable of facing any judicial punishment coming to him." In other words, I would not suffer greatly if I had to go to the brig.

The CO gave me three choices: to accept an undesirable discharge for the good of the service, or an undesirable discharge for drug abuse, or to face the special court martial for being AWOL for five months. Then he appointed me a military lawyer from the navy, saying that I should talk to him before I made a decision and that I had one week to decide.

I had expected as much, but Ron was very shaken by the CO's decision. Ron said he would help with my court martial if that was what I decided to do. In the meantime, I was assigned to a casual company, a transit unit of men awaiting transfers or discharge orders, on Treasure Island. At least I wasn't being jailed.

I talked to the military lawyer the next day, and he said I had a good chance of getting a general discharge, which is under honorable conditions, if I chose to be court-martialed. He said my combat record and performance would weigh heavily in my favor. He also informed me that I could get the maximum sentence for going AWOL from a combat zone. The maximum is six months in the brig and a bad conduct discharge. A bad conduct discharge is under other than honorable conditions and is second only to a dishonorable discharge, which is the worst a person can get. He also gave me a rundown on what it would mean if I accepted either of my other two alternatives. I talked to Ron about my choices, and he thought I should take my chances with a court-martial also. Despite their advice I decided to take an undesirable discharge for drug abuse. I would take my chances upgrading to honorable conditions later through the discharge review process. I had had enough, and this was going to get me out of the military sooner than any other option I had. Of course, it also meant that I was ineligible for VA benefits of any kind.

After I formalized my decision, I was told all such discharges had to be approved by somebody in Washington. It would take thirty days for my discharge to be made final. In the meantime, I was to continue on with the casual company. My duties were mostly cleaning up the barracks and picking up litter around Treasure Island. I was also free to go on liberty almost every night. With my parents living in Redwood City, about thirty miles away, I would go home and return by morning for muster at 7:30 a.m.

One day, after finishing my duties, I lay down on my rack

for a nap. I was fully clothed and lying on my back with my arms behind my head, my legs crossed, and my hat tilted down over my eyes with the bill resting on my nose. The guy who was working with me napped a few racks over. I was half asleep when I heard rapid footsteps coming into the barracks. The other guy jumped clean out of his rack when the feet approached him. Without moving, I peeked through the space between my face and the bill of my hat to see who it was. It was our NCO, a marine who had never left the United States. I didn't have much respect for him as an NCO. He yelled at the other guy, asking him what he thought he was doing taking a nap, and the guy said that I had said it was okay. I didn't move an inch. The corporal walked up to the foot of my rack and whispered to the other guy, "Watch this," and he stepped back and kicked the bottom of my boot. I jumped out of the rack and gave him an uppercut to this balls. He fell to the ground unable to talk, holding his crotch. Then I gathered some of my things, walked out of the barracks into another barracks, changed into my civilian clothes, and caught a bus into San Francisco.

The casual company staff NCO called my folks and told them if I showed up there, they should call the Shore Patrol MPs or him. My parents said they would, but of course they didn't. I was AWOL again, this time for fourteen days. I turned myself in, realizing I was only compounding my problems by staying AWOL.

This time I was facing office hours, the lowest level of the military judicial process. Office hours are presided over by the company's highest-ranking staff NCO. In my case, he was an E–8, a master gunnery sergeant. I was written up for assaulting an NCO and for being AWOL for fourteen days. The sergeant busted me down to private, fined me a month's pay, and gave me thirty days in the brig. The sentence was the maximum afforded him through office hours. He said the charge of assaulting an NCO was dropped because if he let it stand, I would have to face a summary court-martial instead of office hours. He also said he dropped the charge because he thought it was stupid for the NCO to get anyone's attention that way, especially a combat veteran's.

I was taken to the brig that day and served the entire thirty-day sentence. Apparently my discharge had been approved, but they wouldn't process me until I finished my sentence.

After being released from the brig, a marine MP escorted me through my entire discharge process. He said our CO wanted it that way. I asked the MP if I could make one more purchase at the PX, the commissary store, before I left the base for good. First he said no, then, just before we were ready to part at the gate, he turned around and let me buy what I wanted: a navy flight deck jacket that would have cost me double on the outside. The MP made sure I boarded the civilian bus just outside the gate.

This is a fitting departure, I thought as we pulled away. I was almost prideful that it had turned out this way. The Vietnam War was such an injustice, it was only fitting that I not feel any honor in my status. What I had participated in was dishonorable in the truest sense of the word. And maybe I had received what I deserved. At least for the time being.

Part Three

AFTER

Viet Nam and El Salvador,
and on and on forever . . .

I was seventeen and lost
when I met a man, much older and much more lost
who turned me into a pair of ears to hear
the way the world really is —
how the men in power sent younger, helpless men
into a real-life horror movie
with monsters of bullets and mines and unseen
    hands
popping out to kill and maim them for real,
    without
reason or sense or plot,
and worse, to be made into killers themselves,
the visions of that to haunt them forever.

When I was much older, and much more lost,
a seventeen year old boy sat in my classroom
and said, "I think we should go on down
and show those spics what democracy's all about."
And I knew that we are all much too lost
to ever make sense of the world again.

Renny Christopher

Nine

BACK IN THE WORLD, 1971

After seventeen months in Vietnam and three years in the Marine Corps, I finally was out of the military.

My mother was worried about me. "Son, what's the matter with you? You've been out now three months, and all you've been doing is drinking wine and smoking pot. Don't you think you should go out with girls now? And don't you think you should get a job or something?"

"I have a job, Mom."

"You call delivering newspapers by car a job?"

"Okay, okay, I'll look for another job. Or something."

It wasn't exactly in my plans, nor do I think it is what my mother had in mind, but that something manifested itself in a way that seems surreal now.

Late one night, after a night of drinking and experimenting with cocaine for the first time, I was hitchhiking from a friend's house. I was standing across the street from a convenience store, watching the scarce activity come and go. I decided this would be the one, the one that I was going to rob. I didn't do it that night, but just the thought of it was exciting. I hadn't felt that kind of adrenaline rush since Vietnam. It felt good in a twisted way. Even then I knew my feelings came from the fear of potential violence. I had experienced few comfortable feelings since coming home, at least few that were drug free.

I decided to get a toy gun since the clerk didn't seem the type to know how to use a firearm. Besides, if I had a real gun and was threatened, I wasn't sure I wouldn't use it. I knew I didn't want to hurt anyone. Even in the midst of planning such a crime, I never considered the possibility of having to defend myself. This was a game. If I experienced any resistance, I would take flight.

The idea became an obsession, a mission. The money was incidental. Was it as easy as it looked? I cased the store a few nights later for a two-hour time block I thought would be ideal, midnight to 2 a.m.

The clerk was a rotund, pimple-faced young man, perhaps eighteen to twenty years old. Not at all what I'd call formidable. I waited until another customer was ready to be checked out; I thought it would distract the clerk from me. I walked up to the counter with a quart of beer as the previous customer was pulling out of the parking lot. I paid for the beer, turned to walk away, stopped, turned back around, and said, "Oh, I forgot," pulling out my toy pistol and holding it with two hands toward his belly. "Give me all the money in your cash register! Fast, or I'll blow you away!" He stepped back with a look of terror and disbelief on his face. I screamed at him, "I said *fast!* Move! Move! Twenties first!"

"Please don't hurt me." He fumbled with the money, piling it on the counter. I grabbed the money and stuffed it in my jacket pocket and backed out of the store. I ran through a maze of buildings and streets, and then began walking toward a school where I had stashed a sleeping bag on the roof. Because I had made no effort to disguise myself, I was afraid I would be easily identified if I hitchhiked.

When I got on the roof, I just sat there, scanning the area.

My heart was pounding as I wondered if anyone had seen me go into the schoolyard. From my position I could see a full 360 degrees. I would have laughed out loud if I hadn't thought someone would hear me. I pulled out a joint and discreetly lit it by cupping it in my hands, as if I were back in the bush. "Wow, that was so easy," I whispered to myself. I lay flat on my back, looking up at the stars, feeling pleased with myself for the first time in a long time.

I hardly slept that night. The next day I went to a nearby park and found a shady spot, where I slept for a couple of hours. Later that afternoon I finally counted the money, approximately $260. I treated my friends to a night of drinking, pot smoking, and feasting. They asked where I got the money and didn't believe my lie that I had found it. I never told them the truth.

Within two weeks I did it again. This time I robbed a fast-food restaurant. I had noticed it one evening while hitchhiking home from a friend's and cased it the same way as the convenience store. I even patronized the place. Again it was staffed solely by teenagers, easy marks in my view.

The second time was even easier. A young teenage woman and man, neither one older than twenty, collapsed with fear and huddled behind the counter, begging me not to hurt them. Watching them shake so pathetically made me laugh out loud. I opened both cash registers and rifled them, then left through the back door. I ran through the parking lot to an open field of tall grass where I had stashed my sleeping bag. This time the take was about four hundred dollars, and I spent the money the same way — on drugs and alcohol. The robberies were my private little secret, which I enjoyed reliving over and over again in my head. I was amazed at how weak and stupid these kids were. They were the reason it was so easy.

I decided to give it a rest or, as they say in the movies, lay low for a while. About two months later I robbed a hot dog joint. Same situation, same method of operation, same young teenage workers. Again it was not a lot of money, $240 or so, but this time I bought a new ten-speed bike with my take.

My next heist was a little dairy stand, but this time I became much bolder—I performed my deed at eight-thirty in the evening, just before closing time. I had observed the routine a couple of days and thought there would be no problem. The kid who worked there was Chicano, and each night at around nine o'clock someone (I think his father) would pick him up. The area around the store was not dense with buildings, but there were a few houses nearby. The kid was stocking the refrigerator with his back to me as I walked in. "I'll be right with you," he said.

Pointing the toy pistol at him, I yelled, "Now!" He dropped what he had in his hand, juice or something in a little waxed carton. He hurried to the counter, opened the cash register, and began taking the money out. Just then someone drove up, the man I thought was his father. I grabbed what money was on the counter and ran out the entrance.

"He just robbed me!" the kid yelled. The guy in the car started after me on foot. Holy shit, I thought as he started to gain on me. I headed for a series of fences to lose him, and he almost caught me just as I reached the first fence. He was very fast for an older guy. A dog started barking from somewhere. A porch light came on. Now I was scared.

I lost the guy, but I was in a panic as to where to go next. I landed in front of a house that seemed to be empty. I left the yard through a gate, walking slowly and carefully at first so as not to attract attention. Once safely out of the area, I ran.

I realized this game could get very serious. Suddenly the rush and the excitement was not worth going to jail. I vowed to myself and God that I would never do it again. I decided to quit while I was ahead. Ahead about eighty dollars.

Later that first year as a civilian, I stopped at the co-op market on California Street in Palo Alto after delivering my newspapers. I met an interesting man named Larry Trammit. Larry had a United Farm Workers table set up outside the market and was soliciting signatures in support of laws to protect farmworkers. I had a passing awareness of the movement called the UFW National Grape Boycott. In fact, the reason I was shopping at the co-op was that my mother told me it was one of a few stores that sold union grapes and lettuce.

While Larry was trying to convince me to volunteer, I was remembering that my own family was not that far removed from the fields. My parents always considered themselves to be Californians first, Mexicans second, and then Americans. All of my relatives had, at one time or another, worked the fields of California, and some still were working them. My parents had worked the fields as children and from time to time worked at nurseries in the Santa Clara County area to supplement their income. However, *we,* my siblings and I, were never asked to do field work. My father would say, "No son or daughter of mine is going to do wetback work."

When I met Larry that day, I think I felt guilty. This young, bright, enthusiastic man was doing what I should be doing, so I volunteered to help. Plus I thought it would make Mom happy. I worked for the UFW for the next year almost full-time, then for another year and a half part-time.

My work with the UFW was really somewhat of a religious experience, or at least it was the closest thing to one I would have in those days. In many ways it was something I felt compelled to do, not just because it was primarily a Chicano issue or because my family was only one generation removed from the fields. I was looking for something far removed from the war and the violence that I had committed on my heart and soul. The core of the UFW's movement was nonviolence and civil disobedience. Its leader, Cesar Chavez, was a devout Catholic and somewhat of a saint to his people. The movement had very strong ties to the Catholic Church, or at least so it seemed to me. It was a perfect respite for me. Every aspect of it was foreign to my recent life. I was intrigued by all of it: the way it seemed to capture the hearts and minds of so many of the young and passionate college students, its peaceful emphasis. It was as much good as I could find. It seemed the brave and noble thing to do at the time. Maybe it would save me from what I seemed to be becoming.

Mostly I worked the secondary boycott front. I walked picket lines in front of Safeway stores. I sat at information tables in front of friendly stores like the co-ops, soliciting help, money, and signatures. I would even go door-to-door with our message. We had canned food drives, bake sales, benefit dinners, movies and plays, and we had meetings. Lots of meetings. Most of the volunteers were college students — women with long hair and men with beards. Everybody seemed to dress the same — plaid flannel shirts with Levi's and hiking boots. It wasn't hard for me to adapt. I had changed a lot since being voted best dressed my senior year of high school. Back then, I was very particular about the way I dressed. I wore Pendleton shirts and corduroy and denim Levi's, always neatly and carefully pressed myself. I owned several pairs of nice shoes — Hush Puppies and wing tips. I was also always well groomed and seldom had a hair out of place. I used to get my hair cut every ten days and wore the same pomade my dad wore, Yardley's. I thought I was pretty cool. But after I got out of the corps, the preening felt like self-indulgence.

I grew long hair and a beard — a very scraggly, ugly beard that was thin and patchy around the cheeks — with a thick mustache and goatee. I usually kept my hair tied back in a ponytail. I wore cheap plaid flannel shirts and sweatshirts. I still wore Levi's, but they were usually worn ragged and faded. I traded my Hush Puppies for jungle boots and black Keds tennis shoes. I also wore, and still do, the leather navy flight deck jacket I bought from the PX while waiting to be discharged. The jacket was very important to me and is still a source of warmth and comfort even now as I sit here writing.

The jacket was, at that time, my only valuable possession. It also was a kind of shell or coat of armor that shielded me from the outside world. There were times when I found myself sleeping in an abandoned car or in the bushes and I thought, I don't have anything to my name but this jacket, which has kept me warm through a cold night. I swore never to sell or lose it.

One could say my new lifestyle was somewhat austere and sparse. My commitment to the UFW was not unlike a vow of poverty and sacrifice for the betterment of the poor and helpless. My involvement became all consuming to the point that I hardly worked for money anymore, or I should say I hardly made any money delivering newspapers. I certainly did not make enough to afford rent. I would crash at different friends' places, my parents' home, or my parents' car. I ate at my folks' place sometimes, and sometimes I didn't eat. My priorities usually were gas and wine money.

About six months into the boycott movement, I decided to go to school, at Larry's encouragement. I started with the basics: bonehead English, survival math, speech, government, and so on, at Foothill Junior College in Los Altos. I had a couple of false starts. I was in the habit of drinking early in the morning to be able to go to class. Sometimes it worked; mostly it didn't. Somehow I got to the point where I wanted to be a political science major. The Vietnam War had, for all intents and purposes, made me aware of the way political decisions affect people's lives. It was an exposure to worldly issues. The war, along with the racial prejudice I had faced, had provided me with some understanding of my status in this society. Before the war, I didn't think about my experience in a political way. I don't think I would ever have come to understand it if I hadn't gone to war. Now I needed to match my experiences with some education. However, I did not have the language to say this to myself at the time.

In those days I denied I was a Vietnam veteran. I used to say stuff like, "Oh, I was in the military, but I never left the States," or, "I've been traveling around the country," or, "I've been living out of state." I felt ashamed, guilty, and afraid to say otherwise. I decided to commit my life to social change. During the next fifteen years, though, I spent large chunks of time effecting no social change other than by isolating myself either with drugs or by living in the mountains for five years or by disappearing into the underground economy and growing and selling pot.

From late 1971 through almost all of 1972, I attended many potluck and organizational meetings with the UFW. Two of those meetings in particular changed me.

On one of those occasions, I was asked by the staff in Palo Alto to go to a UFW meeting in San Jose. The meeting was held in a very old, grand Catholic church, one of those buildings that from the moment you walk in, you feel the presence of something mysterious and powerful. It wasn't just its magnificent architecture or the beautiful stained glass. It was something else, something warm and safe. I derived comfort from its musty odor. Even with the lights on, the areas where prayer candles were lit and left to burn had an aura to them. It was familiar and magical at the same time. The meeting itself paled in comparison, except for Bob Baron.

A Chicano in his late twenties or early thirties, about five-foot ten and heavyset, Bob dressed just like a longshoreman, although I don't know what, if anything, he did for pay. Bob led the meeting that night, something to do with a large rally planned by the boycott camps. I was very impressed with his style, a charisma straight out of the 1930s labor movement. He was intense and articulate but down to earth. After the meeting we talked. He said he belonged to other politically active groups and thought I might be interested. He told me the farmworkers and other labor organizations needed more Chicano guys like me, and he invited me to his apartment for coffee and talk.

One foot into his apartment, I was taken aback by all the books that filled his walls. It was like walking into a used bookstore. All his tables and some of the floor were covered with piles of pamphlets and overfilled file folders. After a while Bob revealed that he and his wife, Liz, belonged to the American Communist Party. He made sure I understood that his affiliations with the UFW and the ACP were separate. Although each had similar interest and goals, they did not agree on how to achieve them. He also said that the UFW was very careful about keeping its distance from the ACP and asked that I not reveal his activities or his attempt to recruit me. Of course I agreed. I was flattered by his interest in me.

He said the "party" needed more Chicanos and thought I would appreciate their work. My knowledge and interest in communism up to then was mostly from the Marine Corps's point of view. After all, the threat of communist domination in the world was the reason I went to war. However, my perspective had changed after my first deadly encounter with my enemy. No longer could I dismiss them as misguided zealots. It was their tenacity and determination that caused me to wonder exactly what communism was. Communism had become more than an ideal that was contrary to mine, or was it really that different? My talk with Bob was perhaps the first intellectual conversation I ever had with a fellow Chicano. Bob had such heartfelt convictions about what he thought was just and fair; I could only listen in awe. I was probably more impressed with his vocabulary than the content of his message.

I left Bob's house that night with romantic notions about becoming a labor leader or member of the ACP. However, after a couple of meetings and conversations with some of Bob's comrades, I decided it was not for me. I was not convinced of their ability to effect real social change. They spent most of their time arguing and philosophizing. What I did get out of this relationship was the inspiration to pursue more knowledge. Whether it was about communism or whatever interested me, I realized that it was possible for me to handle higher education. Bob showed me it was possible. Mostly self-taught, Bob stood out as a role model. While other colleagues had encouraged me to pursue a college education, as a fellow Chicano, Bob's encouragement meant more to me.

The second life-altering UFW meeting was a staff gathering at which I got drunk and obnoxious. As drunk as I was that night, I could see the concern and fear on people's faces. I decided they were boring and wanted to leave. A good friend and colleague, David, tried to stop me because I was obviously too drunk to drive. I was crashing at a friend's home who lived nearby and thought I could make it easily enough. David offered to follow me home, but being the stubborn drunk I was, I refused his help.

I was stopped by a sheriff's deputy about three blocks from where I was staying. He administered the roadside sobriety test, which, of course, I failed. I admitted I had been drinking but said that I was more tired than drunk and that I lived just down the street, so would he please let me go. He said no and that I would be given a blood test unless I refused. I refused. He grabbed my arm. I resisted. We struggled, wrestling against my car. Another officer drove up just then. Together they wrestled me to the ground, handcuffed me, then started punching me. I spit in one of their faces. Now they were really mad. They pushed and punched me into the police car. Once inside, I went into a rage, kicking the doors and metal mesh guard between the front and back seats. After I was jailed in a holding cell, I was still yelling and carrying on. One of the officers challenged me to come up close to the bars. I stepped up to spit at him, and he pulled out a canister of Mace from behind his back and sprayed me point-blank in the face. As I struggled to clear my face I could hear the door to my cell being opened and a voice saying, "Now you're all ours, you fucking asshole." I was knocked to the floor, and at least two officers began kicking me and hitting me with something, I am not sure what. They were laughing and calling me names while I was being beaten. I remember thinking I was going to die, then they knocked me out.

I woke up the next morning in a different cell. It was very small, with nothing in it but a urinal that looked more like a drain than a pisser. I lay on the floor, wishing that I had died. Blood had crusted around my nose and upper lip. My body ached all over. My ribs hurt when I took a deep breath. I was moved again several hours later and spent the rest of that weekend in jail. I think my parents bailed me out.

Eventually the incident came to a jury trial. I had wrongly decided to challenge the drunk driving because I never did allow them to give me a blood test, so they had no proof I was drunk. I also asked David to lie about my condition. He reluctantly agreed to testify in court that in his opinion, I was sober that night. With the combination of legal help, false testimony, and effective lying on my part, I managed to turn the jury trial into a joke. It degenerated to an even lower level when, after the jury passed a verdict of guilty, the jury was polled. The judge asked each juror, "Is this your verdict?" All the jurors but one answered, "Yes." A woman in her fifties first replied, "Yes." But then she said, "No," then "Yes" again. Then she burst out crying, saying, "No, no, no. This is not my verdict, Judge. I've been intimidated to give this verdict by the rest of the jury." Then minor pandemonium broke out. My few but vocal supporters, primarily my mother, began yelling and accusing the jurors of being racist and unjust.

After the judge restored order, he conferred with my lawyer and the prosecutor. The judge seemed disgusted and frankly, so was I. I felt guilty and ashamed. I had caused this poor woman unnecessary grief and anguish. The judge asked her why she thought I was not guilty. She said she had been influenced by my mother's emotional outbursts during testimony about the beating I'd received in jail. She also believed my testimony. The judge reluctantly asked my lawyer if we wanted another trial. My lawyer was not very enthusiastic about another trial but said he would continue with me if I wanted. I looked around, and most everyone in the courtroom seemed to be in a state of disbelief. The juror in question was still crying. I decided to accept the verdict of guilty, which caused me to lose my driver's license and to be sentenced to community service. I was ashamed of myself. I was particularly concerned about David's participation in my lies. I remember how uneasy he was on the stand, looking at me with pain in his eyes. Somehow I knew he was asking himself if I was somebody the UFW wanted in its ranks.

Besides my drinking, my temper started to interfere with my UFW work, an obvious problem given the organization's commitment to nonviolence. I had tolerated a great deal of abuse from the general public for the better part of a year. Of course, most of it was verbal. It went with the job. After all, we were out there confronting people, whether it was door-to-door or picketing in front of a store. As much as I admired the rest of the staff's ability to keep their cool, I had a hard time relating to their passivity. It was a difference between me and these middle- and upper-middle-class college students.

Once we were on the sidewalk in front a Safeway store holding signs that said, Boycott Safeway, Safeway Sells Nonunion Lettuce and Grapes, Don't Shop Here! We walked up and down the sidewalk from one driveway entrance to the other, sometimes blocking the entrance to the store parking lot. A guy with no intention of stopping came roaring into the driveway as I was walking across. I stopped just in time for him to run over my foot. I became enraged and picked up a rock as he sped through the parking lot toward the other exit. I started running down the sidewalk. My throw thudded into the street. The rest of the picketers were in shock. "Didn't you see the two children in that car?" one of them asked. I had not and said so. I was angry at them for not supporting me in my outrage. They just kept staring at me in disbelief. I had had enough right then and there. Later David said maybe I could just do information and petition table work in front of friendly stores. I appreciated the adjustment, but in my heart I was finished with this high level of commitment.

At the time I was living in a tent behind a friend's house. His roommates were losing patience, and one of them said I scared her. I remember waking up in my tent with a hangover late one morning. I was so depressed, I felt paralyzed. I lay in that cot for most of that afternoon. Occasionally the wind flapped my tent entrance open long enough for me to see the reflection of my tent in the sliding glass patio door. The sight of it sickened me. I realized something had to change that day. I needed a job, and I needed a place of my own. I also needed to take school more seriously. I could not do any of this while I was so committed to the UFW. The sacrifice was over. I packed up everything the next day and temporarily moved in with my parents.

After moving in with my parents, my life did improve somewhat. I started to take school more seriously, and I got a job working at the University of Santa Clara again. I had worked there when I was AWOL and was lucky to get the job back. However, I was still crashing at friends' homes and in my car, with my parents' home as a base. And I continued to drink and use drugs as long as I could afford them. I hardly gave quitting a thought.

Somehow, in spite of my self-destructive alcoholic lifestyle, I was getting by at school. I would often show up at an early morning class already having drunk at least two beers or enough wine to cop a buzz. The booze seemed to give me the courage just to go to class, let alone participate. I had my moments when I actually came off as being bright and articulate, or so I thought. I also had just as many moments when I was a complete jerk and idiot.

Back in the World, 1971   140 | 141

It seemed that just when I started to think school was a waste of time (more like a waste of my drinking time), someone would step out and say something to me about it. In particular, an academic counselor whose name I've forgotten gave me strength that I still draw upon. She was an African-American, a Black Muslim devotee, a member of the Nation of Islam. She was a proud and intelligent person. Her style was somewhat rough and curt, but no less caring for it. She often became angry at me for trying to bullshit her and often reminded me of the opportunity I had and the obligations to my race to do better. More than once she helped me pull myself out of a bad state of mind by saying things like, "This is nonsense, young man. You are your own worst enemy. The white man doesn't have to hold you back. You are doing it for him! I don't want to hear this whining and self-pity. Be strong and deal with what is in your way. I have other students with far more serious problems." It is odd that I can remember her face and words so vividly, but not her name. She was a large, heavy woman who wore native African clothing. When she walked down a crowded hall, people could sense her presence and seemed automatically to get out of her way. To be quite honest, I don't know if she liked me, but she always helped me by saying exactly the right thing at the right time. Maybe it wasn't what I wanted to hear, but it was always what I needed to hear. She also encouraged me to become more involved with MEChA, a Chicano student organization.

As I became acclimated to the school environment, I found out about financial assistance. The financial support helped me get a place of my own and gave me a comfort zone to explore what else school had to offer. I also took a work-study job as a gardener on campus and had another part-time job off campus. I had little time for anything besides school and work.

I periodically attended MEChA meetings, but only as an observer. I was not sure it was something I wanted to do. It looked interesting enough, but I did not have the confidence to jump in. The group of students who ran and dominated MEChA seemed to be preoccupied with campus and student government issues. I was more interested in farmworkers, the antiwar movement, or the civil rights movement. Eventually I become more involved in MEChA after the old guard left. I helped out by raising money on campus. I also helped with the Cinco de Mayo celebration. At some point, I became president of our MEChA club. During most of my short tenure, I struggled to change the direction and focus of our club. I tried to get us involved with other groups on campus like a women's group called Our Sisters, Ourselves and the Black Student Union. I can't say exactly why I did this, other than I felt MEChA needed to be part of a coalition of groups that had similar issues and interests. I also worked very hard at getting MEChA more involved with the UFW cause. Although many of my fellow Chicano students talked a lot about building coalitions and the UFW struggle, very few would do anything about anything. The students active in MEChA during my tenure were, for the most part, interested in the Cinco de Mayo celebrations, sponsoring Latin music dances, and raising money for the club. I had little support for my agenda, and consequently I was compelled to go along with crowd. I quietly finished my commitment.

Frankly, for whatever reason, I often felt disconnected from my Mexican heritage as it related to school, MEChA, or the UFW, even when I went as far as to learn and perform Mexican folk dances in front of hundreds of people. As I danced, dressed like a peasant, I found myself wondering what the hell I was doing. I felt ridiculous.

Many of my peers began calling me Juan during those days, and although I did not feel any soulful connection to my ethnic heritage or my new name at the time, it kind of stuck. It seems strange now, remembering how awkward I felt. For a long time it seemed not to be me. I gradually became comfortable with the new name, but calling myself Juan instead of John was not a simple matter.

I would get a variety of reactions, depending on with whom I was talking. Most Chicano people accepted Juan. However, several Chicano males reacted with hostility, especially if they knew my given name was John and that I could not speak Spanish very well. In fact, many times Chicano men defiantly call me John after I had introduced myself or someone else had introduced me as Juan. "You're not Juan," one man said to me. "You're a wanna-be Juan." I was so hurt that I didn't take issue with him. I *was* confused about my identity. After all, I had always been John.

Mexican nationals or more recent immigrants would sometimes ignore Juan and insist on calling me John; however, I never felt their reaction was hostile. When I asked for a reason, they would laugh and say, "Oh, you're a John," or, "No, no. You're not a Juan, you're from here." I usually wasn't offended. Monolingual English speakers usually would like Juan and make little issue about it one way or the other. Occasionally I would get a question like, "Why would you want to call yourself Juan? You're from here and speak English."

Most of my old friends who only knew John had a problem with Juan. I never made anybody call me Juan. I decided whatever was easiest for others was okay with me. To this day, none of my oldest friends have called me Juan.

My parents reacted with confusion to Juan. My mother thought out loud, "How peculiar; this is interesting," but ignored it and went on calling me what she and everyone else in the family always called me, Squinch. My aunt Theresa gave me the nickname because I squinted a lot. I hated it. My father, John, Sr., reacted by saying Juan several times with a different overdone Spanish accent, jutting out his chin and staring at me intently, as if saying, "Did I hear you right?" Or more to the point, "I don't like this, and I'm giving you a chance to change your mind before I get really mad." He finished his act with a disgusted laugh and said, "You're Juan, all right. Oh, great, that goes with the way you look, with that long hair and beard. Just like a wetback!" He also made a remark about me not wanting his name and asked what was wrong with John. I remember my answer, "John is your name. I'm not you!" He asked if I was going to legally change it. I said maybe, I didn't know. Again he smirked and laughed in disgust, using intonations and facial expressions only I or someone in the family could read. I knew I had pissed him off, but I didn't care. I was angry at my parents for more than just this Juan thing.

I was becoming increasingly resentful about my loss of the Spanish language. Being more involved with Spanish speakers in school and work was causing me to face this shortcoming. I got a lot of mixed messages about Spanish, which is really my second language. I was embarrassed and ashamed to speak Spanish with anyone other than family. Whenever anyone else would speak Spanish to me, I would get a huge rush of anxiety. I would struggle and stammer, feeling inadequate and stupid. Sometimes I would be paralyzed, even if my response required only the most elementary Spanish. Spanish classes were the worst, in high school and college. Rather than excel, I would barely get by. I had such a hard time of it in high school that I not only failed in at least two classes, I was actually suspended from a Spanish class for harassing the teacher. In college I struggled through and got Cs.

When I think back on it, I wonder how I managed to go to college full-time, what with work and all my drinking and drug abuse. I did, though, and with a B average. My success in school was due in part to the influence of Bob and of my counselor. Also, in some way I think I was able to draw some strength from a woman I had met and fallen in love with just before I started school.

Her name was Brigette. We met one day when I was hitchhiking on El Camino Real. Brigette was from Stuttgart, Germany. She had married a Chicano GI while he was stationed there. They had two sons when they came to California to build their lives but later divorced.

I'll never forget that first awkward meeting. While driving along, her boys in the car with us, we shared small talk. I sensed the mutual attraction, but I was unable to respond. All of my relationships with women since getting out of the military had been purely superficial, for sex only. At least from my side of it. I wasn't looking for a lover.

After she dropped me off, I saw her turn into the parking lot of a nearby shopping center. While I was hitchhiking, I thought, What a dummy I am! That girl is beautiful. Why didn't you ask her for a date or something? It's obvious she likes you. I turned down a ride and went looking for her car in the parking lot. It wasn't hard to find. It was a bright red 1952 Triumph TD, beautifully restored. I waited by the car until they came back. She was intrigued and flattered by my detour. She gave me her number.

The prospect of being able to date this woman had given me hope that maybe the Vietnam War wasn't stamped on my forehead after all, and even if it was, I didn't care. I felt good about myself. I felt alive and happy in a way I hadn't felt in a long time.

Brigette was a "rugged individualist." When I met her, she had her own home and a small sewing business that provided her and her sons with a good life. Our relationship grew because we shared many beliefs about social change in the world. Eventually I felt I could trust her with my secret about the war. At first she was angry that I hadn't told her sooner, but she said she understood why I kept it in. She explained that Germans were no strangers to war and its effects. Her father had died in World War II. Germany was changed forever because of the mistakes of a few people. I knew it was far more than a few people, but I didn't argue. She was bitter about what the war had done to her and her country. She was a victim of war as I was, and because of it I felt I had a cohort as well as a lover, someone who more than loved me . . . someone who *understood* some of the pain I carried. It was a tremendous relief for me.

Eventually we grew in different directions. Our parting had mostly to do with my inability to grow up fast enough for her. I think about her often and wonder if she has any idea of how she helped and influenced me.

I transferred to the University of California at Santa Cruz in September 1974 with the aspiration of getting a bachelor's degree in political science, then going on to law school. When I first arrived, I had no friends or acquaintances. I went to the equal opportunity program office, hoping they could help me find a roommate, preferably a Chicano veteran who wanted to live off campus. In a sense, this was my first attempt at reaching out to the part of me I had denied, my veteranhood.

The people at EOP thought my request was strange and unreasonable, but they found someone almost immediately. Ray, my new roommate, had been a medic in the army and was going through a premed program. He was a good student and a quiet man, in many ways an ideal roommate. He didn't smoke or drink a lot, didn't have a lot of people coming over or loud parties or loud habits. He was mild mannered and conservative.

One day Ray was sitting on the end of his bed, sketching with charcoal. I walked into his room and watched him draw a shadowy, ghostlike man wearing a hat and coat. He said the man's image had come to him the night before, waking him from his sleep. He didn't know if the man was a ghost or from his dreams. I told Ray I thought his drawing was good. He seemed surprised that I thought so. It was actually the first time I had ever seen his work. He was usually more private about it. Soon after he refocused his studies to art.

Our conversations were usually political and philosophical

in nature. We both avoided talking about the war, and I didn't mind. Ray and I were quite different, almost opposites. Ray was much more mature and at peace with himself than I was. Eventually he moved into a place of his own. I was becoming more and more depressed about school. I wasn't adjusting to the academic freedom at UCSC, where there were no grades and less structure than at Foothill. I was used to more accountability.

After a quarter at UCSC, I decided to try a double major in community studies and politics. The decision only compounded my problems. I was becoming more withdrawn and depressed. I started drinking heavily and using drugs intravenously again. I was lonely and sad all the time. My only relief was staying high. I started hanging out with a couple of guys whom I had met through Ray. They were Chicano artists who had dropped out of UCSC. They also were drug addicts and criminals who had done time for possession, drug sales, and burglaries. Their names were Jesús and Hector. Both of these guys liked to party, and eventually it killed Hector when he overdosed. We drank, shot up drugs, and terrorized the students on campus by crashing parties and fighting. I also returned to my criminal ways with them, rolling people for money and selling dope.

Around the same time, I became involved with a young Chicana student, Julia. I actually tried to work at this relationship, however awkward and weak it was. Frankly, I was somewhat surprised at her interest in me. Although we had similar backgrounds, hers was much more stable, and it showed in her maturity. She was intelligent and focused on her education. She was passionate about everything she did, involving herself in many different political issues of the time. She was fascinated with my experiences in the war and was the first woman since Brigette who I confided in, sharing some of my deepest hurts and concerns about what I had experienced.

Julia wanted to understand. It was one of the times in my life when I was truly ready and hungry for female understanding. Sitting with Julia in her car many nights, sometimes talking long into the early morning, I began to heal, but I didn't know it then. Her beautiful brown eyes opened wide as I confessed the moral and civil violations I had committed. My criminal activities, including the recent acts of crime at the university, fascinated her.

She had no experience in matters of the street, such as hard drugs, crime, or violence. Like me, Julia came from a family of upwardly mobile, working-class suburbanites. Unlike me, she had a very strong command of her Spanish. But no matter how hard she tried, she couldn't shake that preppie coed veneer. She might have fooled others, but I knew her like I knew part of myself.

Eventually Julia became dubious about me — my absence from classes, my heavy drinking. The final straw was when she witnessed a fight at a party. She was very disturbed at my meanness. She also said that she didn't think I would change. Although I truly hoped for a meaningful relationship with her, I didn't press her for another chance. I believed she was too good for me and didn't want to make a fool of myself by pursuing her. At the time she was right about me. I simply was not capable of that kind of relationship.

Going to school, working, and abusing myself with drugs was not working the way it had worked before. I was falling behind, and I didn't care. I was giving up. I felt lost in this school in the woods. Compared to Foothill, it seemed almost apolitical.

In spring quarter 1975, my third quarter at UCSC, I took a politics course called The Southeast Asian Wars (Vietnam). The small class was taught by a teaching assistant. At first I was skeptical and afraid, but I felt drawn to the class. I knew I could not sit through it without revealing my veteran status, but it seemed worth the risk because I wanted to know how other people felt now. Maybe I was trying to find out how I felt?

The class went fairly well for about three weeks. I admitted to being a veteran and tried to contribute the best I could. Of the eight to ten people in the class, more than half were women. The atmosphere was high energy, charged with hot antiwar passion. I loved it. It was encouraging me out of my depression about being at this "parklike" place called a school.

At the start of the fourth week, we watched a documentary made in North Vietnam. Except for in my dreams and memories, it was the first time I had seen civilian victims and casualties since leaving the war. They were images I had wanted to block from my consciousness forever. The children running and screaming from napalm burns evoked such pain and memories. I wanted to cry, but I didn't let myself. Most of the rest of the class was in tears and silent long after the film ended. I couldn't talk because I knew I would lose control. Finally one of the more impassioned women in the class started yelling, "What's the matter with all of you? How can we just sit here feeling sorry for ourselves? We must talk about what we must do now about this terrible injustice! We must organize to put a stop to it! We must go out and openly protest! Wake up!"

Then she turned to me and pointed her finger at my face. "And you! Of all the people in this class, you know about this inhumanity better than all of us! How can you just sit there with nothing to say about what we have just seen? You've been sitting through this class like it was any other class! Don't you care? Don't you feel *anything?*"

I was hurt deeply, but instead of saying that, I just got angry. I told her she had no right to say those things to me and that she could never understand how I felt even if I did talk about it. Then I stormed out. I never returned. In fact, I dropped out of school altogether, although I did have the foresight to take a leave of absence.

The blasting I had gotten from that woman brought all my guilt and shame about the war to the fore of my consciousness. I could not bear the thought of being confronted again. A part of me knew she was right, and I admired her courage and passion, but there was another part of me that was not ready to face my memories of the war. I didn't know why, so I just copped out.

Ten

ROAD HOME

"There is no boot camp for Viet Nam vets' wives"

In my dream
nothing is the same.
I am running,
my feet striking the ground and lifting,
but never fast enough,
never fast enough.
Chasing me is a monster
with the eyes of a man
and the hands of a wolf,
deformed and twisted claws
at the ends of long arms.
When he smiles
yellow fangs break through his beard.
Spanish moss hangs from trees,
reaches out to me in living tendrils
to hold me back,
but I break through, run on,
reach the cliff edge and turn,
my back to the open sky
while my feet dance, wanting to leap over,
but I stay, stay,
and the beast approaches
eyes red in the night.
I open my arms, bare my neck,
stretch out against the night,
and on he comes.
I awake with pounding heart
and shallow breath.

He lies beside me
with the eyes of a man
and the hands of a man,
but still I am afraid,
afraid to move, for fear of
arousing the monster.
In the world of waking,
nothing is the same.

Renny Christopher

For the next couple of years I did gardening on the side and worked part-time in a bar down by the wharf. I also worked in a fiberglass boat shop. I made a lot of friends and acquaintances at the bar and the boat shop, friends I feel fortunate to still have. Of all the lasting friendships I made while working at the bar, the most significant was with the woman who would become my wife.

Linda was the best friend of one of my coworkers at the bar. She wasn't the kind of woman I was used to dating. In a sense, she was a purist. She ate no meat or sugar or anything else she felt was unhealthy. She was petite, soft, and innocent. When I was first introduced, although she was attractive, I didn't feel we had anything in common. It didn't occur to me that she would be interested in me. She seemed out of place in the bar, with her long brown hair, colorful "flower child" fashions, wire-rimmed glasses, and serene nature. We were opposites. As much as I liked her, I didn't really consider the possibility of a relationship with her. But that's not how it turned out, although the evolution of our relationship was slow and careful.

I best remember the relationship as a welcome relief to how I was living. Linda wasn't a drinker or drug user. When I was with her, I did my best to behave. I worked hard at concealing my drinking problem from her. She never pressed me for a commitment, and I appreciated that. Even though I was still abusing drugs and alcohol, I was trying to make a change. My exposure to Linda's personality was encouraging that change. I was trying to be somebody more like her. Someone who was mature and at peace with himself.

Before meeting Linda, despite the fact that I was always employed in some way or other, my life was full of despair and wastefulness. I had wholeheartedly resorted to the lifestyle I had had just after getting out of the military. When substance abuse interfered with work, I usually was allowed to "slide" because most of the time I had good work habits. I lived to work and get high — at a dangerous level. I had had various alcohol and drug-related criminal convictions before coming to Santa Cruz County, and now I was adding up a few here, too.

Prior to coming to Santa Cruz, I had been convicted of drunk driving twice, assault on police officers, and resisting arrest during barroom brawls twice. I was lucky; I got away with relatively soft sentences. I also was lucky not to be caught committing the other, more serious crimes I was entertaining myself with. But I didn't and still don't perceive myself as a hardened criminal. I always have been willing and able to work for my money. I just committed crimes for the excitement, pure and simple. Sometimes I would even pull "ambushes" on people who had slighted me, following them and then surprising them: "I'm the guy you cut off ten miles back," or, "I'm the guy you tried to cheat out of money," or, "I'm the guy you fired or harassed when I worked for you." Sometimes I would assault the person, but usually I was satisfied to terrorize them.

After leaving UCSC, I had resorted to similar but not as severe behavior, the worst being drinking until I blacked out and brawling in unfriendly bars. One time I got so drunk that I broke into what I thought was my house and slept the night there. Luckily no one was home. In total, I was arrested and convicted for drunk driving, assault, and disturbing the peace — once each.

Although Linda was around when I was banished from the

bar for fighting, I believed she had no idea just how severe my problems were. Since leaving school, I no longer denied being a veteran, but I still refused to discuss it at any length. In fact, it was a considerable amount of time before I brought the subject up with Linda. I think I slid over it so fast that I don't even remember when I did tell her, but I'm sure it was months after we met.

After about a year, I realized I loved Linda and wanted to be with her for the rest of my life. We were at an ice-cream parlor and I was watching her from across the room as she stood in line to order. At that moment she seemed almost angelic to me, standing there patiently, a soft smile on her face. I thought, Of course! How did I not see it before? This woman is what I need and want to be happy! So I asked her if she wanted us to live together, and she said yes.

Our life was good for about a year. I drank, but I didn't abuse it to the point that it interfered with our relationship. Linda seemed to tolerate the alcohol and other drugs as part of our personal differences. We both understood that we were very different. But I think we appreciated the differences rather than resenting them. After that first year, though, I started drinking heavily again. I would drink about two six-packs of beer a night without getting too drunk. Sometimes, at least once a week, I'd stay out drinking until the bars closed. Sometimes I'd stay gone all day and night, sleeping in my truck or at a friend's house. Then if I did make it home after drinking all night, I'd start in on Linda, keeping her up, raging at her about everything, threatening her with violence. Sometimes I'd call her up and tell her I would be home in ten minutes. Then I wouldn't show. A couple of times I called threatening her with talk of suicide.

I'd go through two or three weeks of this outrageous behavior, then something would happen. I'd get into a terrible fight, or I'd black out and not remember what I had done or where I'd been. Once I crashed my truck and luckily didn't hurt anyone except myself. Sometimes I'd get up screaming, half drunk and, in the middle of a nightmare, attack Linda in bed, or get up and walk around the house in my sleep looking for intruders. Sometimes I went outside at night naked.

Linda would tell me about the horrible things I said and did. I could hardly believe her because I never remembered the incidents. She'd say it was as if I were a completely different person. She said that the other person I transformed into was evil and mean, that my face distorted with vicious expressions of anger and rage. I would feel ashamed and guilty and try to convince her that I was sorry, that I would try to *control* my drinking. Each time she would accept my remorse and regret as sincere. I'd be a good guy for about a month or so, and then slowly start the cycle again. Each time Linda lost more and more respect for me and for herself. Each time I would tear off a layer of her innocence and patience. Finally she said that if I didn't stop drinking or seek help, she would ask me to leave.

First I tried it on my own. I stayed sober for a while, but sneak drinking always led to binges. I entered a rehabilitation program in Santa Cruz. It was the first program I attempted on my own. I had been through alcohol awareness programs before, but only under court order. This one was helpful and a good start for me, but it only worked temporarily. Later I checked into the Community Counseling Center for Drug Abuse. My counselor was a woman who was also a marriage counselor. Her name was Joanna Kranich.

Somewhere along in the early stages of my therapy the subject of my being a combat veteran came up. Joanna told me she was working with a veterans' peer group as a cofacilitator. The other facilitator was a combat veteran himself. She said she thought I might be interested. I already knew about the group because when I was looking for employment through Veterans' Outreach, David Heaston, the vocational counselor, told me about it. I went on to tell her the same thing I had told Dave, that I was not troubled in the least by my participation in the Vietnam War. My problems stemmed from being an alcoholic and violent long before going to Vietnam. From Dave and Joanna's reaction, I knew they doubted the war issue was really settled for me. But they didn't press me to go. However, they both convinced me to at least talk to the peer counselor, Mark Sandman, on the telephone.

My attitude about the war then was not to deny I had been there but to explain it away as bad history better forgotten. I had a lot of opinions about it but wouldn't necessarily volunteer them. If the subject did come up in conversation, I would say what I thought — vehemently. If something would come on the television about the war or veterans, it used to make me angry, almost instantaneously. I had the same reaction to movies about the war.

I continued my therapy with Joanna, trying to get to the root of my substance abuse. Linda and I also started marriage counseling with Joanna. For a whole year, Mark periodically called me up and asked if I were ready to attend the veterans' peer group, and I always said no. Joanna also occasionally reminded me about the group, but I always said no.

Although I was still going on and off the wagon, I was getting more serious about changing my life. When I turned thirty in 1979, I said to myself, "Well, looking back on my thirty years, I don't have much to show for it," and I decided that it was about time I grew up and started acting like a man. One of the things I decided to do was marry Linda.

The idea took her by surprise and she was reluctant, thinking it might only make things worse. She asked me why I wanted to get married. I'd had a philosophy teacher at Foothill who said people ought to live together for five years before they got married. We'd been living together for four years, and that seemed close enough. Also, I'd always figured I wouldn't get married until I was thirty, and now I was. Most important, I told her I wanted to have children, and I thought we should be married before we had children. She finally said yes.

One other event about this time distracted me from my self-destructive behavior. I helped form a union at a small, local leather belt and wallet factory where I worked from 1977 to 1980. Dave Heaston from Veterans' Outreach had helped me get the job at Lazy Day Leathers, with a good recommendation. Lazy Day was an easygoing, kicked-back place to work and paid "good wages for Santa Cruz." It was the longest full-time job I had ever held.

Although reluctant at first to get involved, I began to see the union as a way to make a place for myself, a place of my own creation. I also think I was bored with the routine of the factory, and this endeavor seemed more exciting than anything else that was going on there or in my personal life. After a sluggish start, we eventually voted to unionize. We created our own constitution and bylaws, elected representatives, and made contract proposals and negotiated directly with the company's management people. We had weekly meetings and conducted expedient grievance procedures.

However, it didn't last. The company was having such financial difficulty that they decided to move to San Antonio to take advantage of Texas's "right-to-work" laws and a cheap labor pool. We won our election in February 1980. By December 1980 the last of us were laid off permanently.

Participating in the union drives and eventually becoming the president of our own independent union stirred my passion for being involved with issues of social change again. I was confident that despite the impending layoff, I could do wonderful things if I really wanted to. I was even excited at the prospect of being laid off. I knew it would force me to make changes. In a sense, it was a blessing. Being involved with the union work was also a long period of sobriety.

I was now on unemployment insurance for the first time in my life, and I didn't like the feeling or the stigma. I went back to Veterans' Outreach to see if Dave could help me get a job. Even though my discharge status was not honorable, Dave bent the rules to help me. Dave was instrumental in getting me two jobs, one driving and then one making adobe bricks. After being laid off, though, I was back on unemployment benefits and eventually wound up simultaneously working for "under-the-table wages" at all sorts of jobs — concrete pumping, cement work, house repairs, landscaping. In fact, after leaving Lazy Day Leathers in December 1980 I worked exclusively in what is referred to as the "underground economy" and did very well with it for several years. I began doing so well that I even stopped drawing the unemployment checks because it got to be more hassle than it was worth, and I was scared I would get caught. I even managed to save money. I saved enough periodically to buy gardening equipment. Slowly I built up a gardening maintenance clientele.

Even though my economic status was relatively comfortable, I was playing games with my attempt at sobriety. I was fooling almost everyone. But Linda knew. She knew because every now and then I would go somewhere out of town and get drunk and then come home raising hell. These incidents were becoming less and less frequent, but I was still causing a lot of damage to our relationship. It was almost as if Linda didn't care anymore. Not even the long periods of stability mattered to her. She was fed up. Each time she became less trusting of me, in general less sympathetic and less understanding.

I was stuck in my therapy with Joanna and finally agreed to try out the veterans' peer group sessions. I still didn't like the idea, but I couldn't ignore the way Linda was changing. When I first started the group, I think Linda was a little worried about bringing my veteran issues to the fore. Within the previous year, she had seen me resort to the Vietnam War as an excuse for my repeated regressions into drunkenness. I had run out of excuses for these setbacks. Because the media and the public had the perception that *all* Vietnam veterans were not playing with full decks, I figured I could get some mileage out of it, too. In fact, while I was in counseling, I would get distraught and depressed over any negative news involving the war or Vietnam veterans. One night after listening to a story from one of the guys in our group about an accidental shooting of a civilian, I decided to get drunk. I was very affected by the story, and drinking only made things worse. I called Linda from a telephone booth and told her I was going to kill myself. I went home first, to increase the drama, and gave some speech about what I had done and what I deserved because of my actions. Then I told Linda that I was going to run right off the sea cliffs just three blocks away, and I ran out of the house. She followed me, crying and screaming for me to stop. I ran up to the edge of a cliff and stood there with my feet half over the edge. I told her not to try to get any closer or I would jump. She was terrified. The wind was strong and gusty, blowing the spray from the surf into my face. The exhilaration of the moment sobered me up enough to realize what I was doing to this poor woman whom I supposedly loved. What has she done to deserve such treatment, I thought. Then, just for an instant, If I relax, maybe a strong gust of wind will blow me over without me having to get the courage to jump. Looking at Linda, I thought I should really do it this time for *her* sake; I'd ruined her life. I soon realized how stupid and evil this display was. We went home together.

I didn't use my status as a veteran to explain my bad behavior to anyone else except Linda, because she was really the only person in my life confronting me with my alcoholism. For the next year and a half, I periodically attended the group sessions and continued my therapy with Joanna on and off.

I remember those first twelve to twenty-four weeks well because it took me that long before I decided to use the veterans' group sessions seriously. I was angry, hostile, and distrusting of the group in general and refused to cooperate at first. I listened, though, and often felt that most of the guys in the group indeed were blaming the war and the rest of society for all their problems. It was exactly what I had thought it would be: a crying and sniveling session. I said as much when the group started pressuring me to participate more. I'll never forget that moment because it was the beginning of what has turned out to be my ongoing recovery from alcoholism and the trauma from the Vietnam War. When confronted by the group, I lashed out: "I don't have the same problems as the rest of you guys in here. I knew what I was getting into when I enlisted. Maybe some of you who were drafted have an issue with the government and society, but I enlisted. I chose to participate. I knew there was a war going on, and I knew I would be in combat and knew what might happen! For me and those like me, we got what we expected. It was war! People kill, people die! Some get hurt for the rest of their lives, but that's what war is about! Killing and dying! What right do we have to sit around here feeling sorry for ourselves when the country we violated with this injustice is still in a state of agony? I have problems, all right, but I don't think they came from what I did in Vietnam. I'm fucked up because I drink too much and then get violent. I might even have a chip on my shoulder about being a Mexican. I survived the war and so did you guys, so why sit here and whine and snivel about it? It's history. It's over! I made my peace with what I did by accepting that it was wrong to be a part of it in the first place. Any pain I have from it is my due until God sees fit to release me from it. No one else is going to do it; it's between me and God, and that's it!"

"Well, if that's the way you feel, good for you," said Mark. But he and Joanna disagreed with my use of the words *whine* and *snivel*. Most of the guys also took offense, and they let me know about it. I expected as much. But when Dennis, a fellow veteran whom I grew to respect, carefully explained that the "whining" and "sniveling" was actually a kind of healing process, I actually apologized for the tirade. His words had touched me.

I went home that night with a great sense of relief. I had said what I needed to but also realized I was more hurt and angry about the war than I was willing to admit, even to myself. If guys like Mark and Dennis, who had experienced combat as severe as I had, could talk about it and understand themselves as *victims* as well as *perpetrators,* then maybe my experience in Vietnam *was* traumatic and maybe I *had* "stuffed it," hoping it would somehow go away.

I began to understand my experience in a new way. What I eventually came to believe, what I still believe, what finally allowed me to come to livable terms with my experience, was this: I, and all the other young Americans like me, were victimized by the U.S. war machine, which played on our honest patriotic desire by lying to us about the nature of the war. At the same time, we are morally responsible for our own actions in the war. This insight eventually allowed me to admit the traumatic nature of my own experience without "letting myself off the hook" for anything I did. It became possible for me to feel bad about some of my own actions but also to admit that I had the right to feel bad about what had been done to me by my government.

I started to have more compassion for my peers and tried to put myself in their shoes instead of looking at them as complainers. I started to understand the problems of Vietnam veterans in an intellectual way but not in a personal way. In other words, I took on the role of a peer counselor to protect myself from *real* self-evaluation and scrutiny of my own trauma.

The veterans who participated in these groups came from many different strata of society. They were bonded together in this "safe" place only because of their shared experiences in Vietnam. Camaraderie was important to members of the group, but especially to me. I never had comradeship with other veterans during or after the war. Some of my problems stemmed from racial conflicts early in my combat career. I wasn't black, and I wasn't white; I wasn't Chicano enough for some, and I certainly wasn't the hero type of marine that many of my Chicano peers felt *they* were. Early on I lost acquaintances before they turned into friends because of our inexperience and the intensity of the war. In addition, because I was wounded and separated early on from my original combat group, I decided to be concerned only with myself and "to hell with the rest of these dumb motherfuckers." Being close to someone was dangerous because that person might die. Being close to someone was dangerous because I might sacrifice my life for that person. I never had a true buddy except one, Peanuts, and that didn't last, either.

In the veterans' support group, I still tended not to let people get too close to me, but I had come to respect my peers. I felt guilty about things I used to say about some of my peers, especially those who didn't survive. That's what they get for being heroes or just plain stupid, I used to think. The guilt toward my peers was different than the surface, conscious guilt about the war. On the surface I felt guilty about perpetrating violence on the Vietnamese people. Deep inside I felt guilty about surviving the war when others, more deserving of life, had not.

In a way this might explain why I helped the newcomers to the group to the point of sacrificing my own personal progress. It was difficult to see at the time because I felt too good about being able to help out, but I confused being helpful with being "well and adjusted." The evidence that I was not adjusted mounted with my behavior outside the group.

I was still engaging in periodic self-destructive behavior such as getting blind drunk, getting into fights I had no chance of winning, or driving at high speeds in the middle of the night. Afterward I would wake from this almost dreamlike state wondering what had possessed me. Why couldn't I be happy and at peace? Although I was very actively trying to help others with their problems, I didn't know how to ask for time. Worse, I didn't think I *deserved* the time to work on myself in the group. Maybe I was throwing up a smoke screen to avoid it. But I was growing more convinced that I was avoiding helping myself because I still didn't feel worthy.

I left the group after about a year, thinking I had gone as far as I could. Before I left, though, I let it out that I had received an undesirable discharge. I felt a great deal of regret about my discharge status. I had been lying to myself about not caring. Most of the guys in our group didn't have bad discharges; I was ashamed. When I told the group about my "bad paper," to my surprise no one belittled me or even expressed bad feelings about people like me. Some guys even encouraged me to go through the appeal process because I *deserved* vindication. Their reaction meant a lot to me. It wasn't just my family or friends saying I should be exonerated. This time it was my *peers*.

Dave Heaston at Veterans' Outreach helped me get the appeal process rolling. He had been trying to get me to do this for a long time. He said the process could take as long as two years, and along the way I was probably going to be denied, but that I should persevere because I had a good case.

Dave referred me to a private, nonprofit organization in San Jose called The G.I. Forum. The G.I. Forum, a Chicano veterans' organization started right after World War II, provided free legal services. The first step was to ask the discharge review board to review my case solely through documents. I could submit a personal statement, my military records, character references, and any other documents I felt were pertinent. This first step took almost a year, and in the review board's own language, I was "denied relief" by a panel of five retired officers, just what Dave had warned me about. I took the slight very hard and gave myself the excuse to get drunk and make Linda miserable. Each time there was a setback or delay, I did the same thing.

The next step was to request a hearing in person. I got a

hearing date within six months. Larry, the lawyer at The G.I. Forum who was helping me with my case, said that I had a good chance for an upgrade at the hearing. I had good proof of post-traumatic problems from when I first tried to get out on a medical discharge. We both felt confident. Unfortunately Larry forgot to send a letter of confirmation. It would be another year before I got another hearing date. And this time I would have to travel to San Diego. My original hearing was to be in San Francisco. To make matters worse, when the hearing drew near, Larry said he could not travel to San Diego with me. One of the lawyers out of their Los Angeles office would present my case instead. Larry told me not to worry; the guy in Los Angeles was quite competent, and anyway, my own record and testimony would be the most important part of my case. I called The G.I. Forum office in Los Angeles, but the guy presenting my case was too busy to meet with me before. Don't worry, he said, I've done thousands of these kinds of cases. The lawyer's name was Anthony Olivia, a Chicano veteran. Tony seemed confident enough over the telephone, but I was worried.

I arrived in San Diego the night before the hearing. I was scared. Because of Larry's fuckup, the next day would be my last chance to appeal. I rented a hotel room near the base, which was also near the airport. From my window I could see the training area where I had gone through boot camp.

Old and sad feelings kept coming up as I sat in that hotel room, looking at the marine training area. My life had changed so much since the last time I was here. I had been so young and cocky then. I remembered how Sergeant King had broken my will. I remembered those first few days, when I wished I hadn't joined. Days that were so painful to my self-esteem and self-worth. I remembered those who went through training with me. Some I knew were dead. What about the others? What were they doing now? Did they have problems, too? I got sad wondering what it was like for those families whose sons, brothers, husbands, and fathers didn't make it. I was feeling guilty again for surviving. Maybe it would be better if I didn't get the upgrade. Who was I kidding? Even if I did get it, I was never going to feel good about my participation and discharge.

I went out to get some dinner, had a few beers, and then on the way back to the hotel stopped and bought a pint of 151 rum. I had promised myself I wouldn't do this, but I had to do something about my guilt and pain. I also expected to fail at my hearing the next day. I downed the pint in about an hour.

I woke up with a start the next morning. I was fully clothed, lying on top of the still made bed. At least I hadn't overslept. I had about an hour and a half before my hearing. I was hung over and remorseful that I was not at my best. I tried to knock out the hangover with food, coffee, and aspirin, but it only seemed to get worse. I made the fifteen-minute walk to the base and, once there, changed into the clothes I had brought for the occasion.

I was on time, but Tony said it would be better if my case came up last. For the next four hours I sat outside the hearing room and watched Tony handle the six other cases. More than half these guys didn't have a chance at winning their appeals, and Tony told them so. Although The G.I. Forum is a Chicano veterans' organization, they would help anybody with "bad paper." Watching Tony work, I thought, This guy is hard as nails and cold. How's he going to treat me?

Finally it was my turn. Tony warned me that the board consisted of four marine officers (three majors and one colonel) and one navy officer (a commander). He said it could be a bad thing. In his experience, a board stacked with marine officers was usually tough to convince. On the other hand, he said most of these men were probably bush officers when I was in the bush — my combat record might weigh heavily in my favor. He said I had only one reason to be nervous — if I was going to lie. If I told the truth, my chances of getting the upgrade were good.

Tony did a good job introducing my case. Then he handed me the ball, as we had agreed. I filled in the gaps as best as I could remember, explaining circumstances that were not in my records or documentation. After I finished, there was a long pause, then disbelief spread across the faces of all the board members, save one major. His expression didn't change the whole time, and he didn't ask any questions. He just stared at me with a hard, blank look for the entire thirty-five minutes I was in there. He made me very nervous.

Finally the colonel spoke up. "Why did we do this to you? This is a disgrace! You've served in eleven major combat operations, received the Purple Heart twice, meritorious promotions for actions under fire, and other recommendations for medals you never got! What is this, some kind of bad joke?"

"I don't know, sir," I said. I was struggling not to cry. I had forgotten about the medals and the incidents connected to them. Or maybe I had blocked them out. It never occurred to me that any of that mattered to anyone anymore.

Before going into the hearing, Tony had told me that I wouldn't get a decision on my case for about three months. A few minutes after I walked out of the room alone, Tony came out smiling. He sat down beside me and said, "You must have really impressed them because they gave me their decision as soon as you left. In over three thousand cases I've worked, this has never happened. They didn't want you to wait any longer, so they gave me permission to tell you that you've been granted an upgrade all the way to an honorable discharge."

I didn't know how to react. A general discharge under honorable conditions or a general discharge without benefits was all I expected. But not this! An honorable discharge also meant full benefits. I wouldn't let myself be happy. I told Tony I would be more convinced once I saw the official documents from the VA. On my way home, though, I found myself wondering that if lifers could forgive me, then maybe I deserved the upgrade after all.

Within three months, the official letter came. Now I was happy. I had gotten more out of it than I ever hoped. It wasn't a dream anymore. I felt a tremendous sense of relief. I could think about going back to school now because of the education benefits. I spent the next academic year at Cabrillo College taking study-skills classes and fulfilling some requirements in order to get back into UC Santa Cruz.

I finally quit drinking on August 13, 1983, but only after three more serious drunks, each about a week apart. I even shot up speed once before I stopped for good. It's difficult for me to make any sense out of those final drunks. Maybe I was trying to sabotage my success again, still feeling I was not worthy of such a favorable turn of events. Or who did I think I was to pursue an education? Nobody else in my family had done it, so why was I any different or better? Or maybe I was too scared to grow up.

I started up with A.A. for that first three months of sobriety. I also simultaneously started up with the group because I needed all the support I could get. A.A. meetings helped me out a great deal at first, but they didn't have all I needed. For the next year I used the support of the group to stay clean. I was lucky — a couple of older guys in our group from the Korean War were recovering alcoholics themselves. I was impressed with their ability to change at such a late stage in their lives. They served as role models that I didn't have growing up in an alcoholic household. They proved to me that a person could change if he wants to. I wanted to break this pattern of alcoholism. I had made the repeated mistake of thinking I could periodically control my problem. I also made the mistake of thinking I could treat myself, that I could recover on my own. I was wrong. And for the next year and a half I made the mistake of believing that just because I was now sober and "well," all my other problems would disappear. I didn't realize that I had a great deal to undo before I could ever say I was cured.

About six months after I stopped drinking, I was full of energy and enthusiasm for life. I was dreaming and hoping again. I could see a better life for me and Linda. I bulled my way through part of that first year in school, impatient that my progress was too slow. I was in a hurry now. My senses wanted stimulation and satisfaction. I was starved for more, more of everything, and I wanted it fast! It was at times as if all my nerve endings were raw and exposed. Everything and everybody were a source of aggravation for me.

More important, although I was sober, Linda and I seemed to have more difficulties than ever. I felt she was stuck with the old me and wouldn't let go for fear of the usual disappointment. I grew increasingly impatient with her. When I went back to the group with my problem, they helped me realize that in my hurry to get on with my new life, I had forgotten the person who had suffered the most with me. I didn't realize that Linda needed help, too. In a sense, I had created a monster with all the years of abuse, and now that I was recovering, I couldn't understand why she wasn't appreciating it more. Linda eventually started some therapy of her own with a veterans' partners group and individual sessions, and it helped her as much as it had helped me. We worked very hard to change our old patterns of relating to each other. We learned how to relate to the outside world again.

As I proceeded with my own adjustment, I realized that although stopping drinking was the key, it was not the solution to my readjustment or my search for a happier life. Quitting drugs and alcohol brought me a new energy and lust for life, but it didn't mean that I was a well-adjusted combat veteran.

I was preoccupied, almost obsessed, with being a veteran by the time I went back to UCSC in 1984 after a ten-year absence. I had to get it out of my system. To some extent, school presented the perfect opportunity to do so. I chose to work with Veterans' Services as part of my major in community studies. I didn't know what would come of my work with veterans. For all I knew, it could kill me, in a soulful way. But it didn't. My work with veterans was therapeutic as well as educational, despite the fact that the bureaucracy was frustrating and that I wasn't able to do as much as I would have liked.

The primary function of Veterans' Outreach was job-search assistance or vocational counseling. Unfortunately we were providing survival-type jobs as opposed to training opportunities for long-term employment. Most of this had to do with the amount of money and time we had for our clients. It was never enough. I stayed on because I knew the program was trying to address a serious problem: the estimated rate of unemployment for veterans was between 15 and 30 percent in Santa Cruz County. The unemployment rate for all residents of Santa Cruz County during the same period was 7.6 percent.

The program's priority had always been the Vietnam combat veteran, then the in-country noncombatant, then the Vietnam-era veteran (who served during the war but not in-country or off its immediate shores), and then all other veterans. There was a dramatic difference between those veterans who experienced prolonged or severe combat and those who experienced none at all or only peripheral kinds of combat. Of the approximately 2.5 million veterans who served in Vietnam, only about one-third actually experienced combat on any kind of daily basis. Even fewer saw prolonged or severe combat. Most Vietnam veterans participated in support-type roles such as supply, clerical, transportation, communications, and medical; more combatlike support such as air and naval gunfire support; or in-the-field support such as artillery, tanks, and other specialty types of weapons. My point is that a veteran's ability to adjust to life after the war is not generally or exclusively due to combat. Most of our clientele tended to be either era veterans or recently discharged veterans. We rarely assisted in-country veterans and even more rarely assisted combat veterans.

Era and recently discharged veterans tended to come in on their own. With Vietnam veterans we had to do very active outreach. We would try to find them in drug and alcohol rehabilitation programs, in jails, through public announcements on the radio or television, in bars, or through referrals from other state agencies. Also, loved ones called in for their Vietnam veteran who was having a problem coping with life. When we found them, very few veterans would stick around for either vocational counseling or readjustment counseling long enough to get a job. Vietnam veterans were very difficult to reach in the first place, and when we did get them, we couldn't sustain their trust long enough to help them.

Then there were the Vietnam veterans who did come on their own, demanding *immediate* attention OR ELSE! For some reason, a lot of our walk-in Vietnam veterans thought we had, or should have had, anything they needed—food, housing, clothing, and of course a job that paid high wages and started immediately. Usually this type of veteran was never actually in combat but said he was. He also tended to put blame on society for his situation and used his status as a veteran to get whatever he could. In other words, he tried to make people feel guilty enough to give him something.

In short, I grew increasingly frustrated with the work.

One night in group, after I had been on my soapbox about the Nicaraguan and Salvadoran civil wars and our country's participation in them, Mark said to me, as he had before, that I was wasting my anger and frustration on the group. They all knew what I was talking about. Wasn't it really the outside world that needed to hear me now?

Through Veterans' Outreach, I began talking to high school classes about the Vietnam War and what it meant to me. Before I started doing these talks, I had a low opinion of young people. But these students really wanted to know more about the truths of the Vietnam War. They cared. They realized they might be asked to lay their lives on the line someday soon and knew they should think about that. These students asked important and meaningful questions. They showed maturity I hadn't given them credit for. I felt there was hope for the outside world after all. Most important to me, I found a way to use a terrible life experience constructively. Maybe I'd save a few lives through my own example.

The talks inspired me to produce videotaped interviews with veterans about their experiences before, during, and after the Vietnam War. I wanted people to understand what Vietnam vets had gone and go through. But I also thought veterans had a vital perspective on U.S. military involvement in Central America, which was increasing at the time.

While at my field-study placement, I had learned that a great many veterans — from World War II, the Korean War, and Vietnam — believed the U.S. government was attempting to revise the history of the Vietnam War in order to foster aggression against South and Central American socialist states. The U.S. government was retelling the history of the Vietnam War in a way that discounted the will and determination of the Vietnamese people and the arrogance and stupidity of our own leaders. As a country, we were choosing either to ignore the Vietnam War or to convince ourselves that the only thing we did wrong was lose. The movie *Rambo* struck me as a perfect example of everything that was wrong with our country's psychology. *Rambo* attempted to erase our national sense of impotence, helplessness, vulnerability, insecurity, and stupidity. *Rambo* could not be discounted as "just a movie." Its kind of hype was misleading and dangerous. Not only did *Rambo* exploit veterans, it glorified the horror that is war and ignored the physical and emotional cost of real combat. *Rambo* made winning the war the only consideration, ignoring any moral or ethical questions about military intervention in the Third World.

I wanted to offer a rebuttal to this dangerous, socially irresponsible "jingoism" through videotaped interviews with real-life veterans who could share their insight on Vietnam as well as offer constructive and peaceful alternatives to military intervention.

I had intended to use the video as my senior thesis, but my plans changed. When I looked for other community studies theses on the Vietnam War or about veterans, I couldn't find one among the thousands of pages of hard work. I was in need of comparison material, so I decided to jot down a few things about my own experiences. I opened a can of worms. I put the video project on hold and became so involved in telling my own readjustment story that it occupied all my time. Although my story was not unique, I felt compelled to make a statement about the war through my own experiences as a grunt, especially as a Chicano.

I had learned a lot about the war and people like myself while working with Veterans' Services. On the one hand, the work was an extension of my therapy, bringing me back home. On the other hand, although I now had a clearer understanding of what happened to me and other veterans and to our country, I was still indignant over the war. I didn't believe this would ever change. In my thesis conclusion I wrote:

So what does all this mean? And who cares? Why should I care? Why should you care?

What this means to me is this: First and foremost, this is for me and for those like me. It's for those who didn't make it back and for their families. It's for the Vietnamese, Cambodians, Laotians, Hmong, Thais, Montagnards, and all those who suffered directly and indirectly because of the war.

It satisfied my need to make a statement toward a peaceful resolution to our differences with the communist world.

It is a story, told to myself, to help me sort out what happened to me and to others like me. Some people have thought that I simply have had a personal problem and this was my way of working it out. Maybe they are right, but it means more than that to me, much more. But the reader will have to decide, finally, whether this paper is only about my personal problem or whether it also says something about all of us and the society we hold to be so righteous.

The Vietnam War changed my life forever, and I believe it changed us as a nation forever. I don't attribute all of my personal troubles to the Vietnam experience. Some of my problems came from how I grew up and the environment I grew up in, some from living in a racist society that systematically channeled me toward becoming a combat soldier. Brown and black people kill and are killed for a society that still calls us spics and niggers when we get home.

Some of my personal problems come from the fact that my own father had made those same sacrifices in World War II. He gave up his youth, innocence, and finally his soul so that he could come home and continue to be treated like a second-class citizen. He developed problems because of his "personal troubles" with those contradictions. Many others of his generation of veterans took to alcohol because they couldn't sort out what happened to them, either. Of course, alcoholism in World War II veterans manifests itself in all segments of society, not just in people of color like my dad. We live in a country that, on the one hand, says it stands for freedom and democracy that is worth fighting and dying for, and on the other hand, through Christianity, holds that it is wrong to kill or to force others to believe as we do. This is one of the serious contradictions in our society. Did God or Jesus really mean that we could be discriminate with our values, that we could go ahead and kill those who do not believe with us, then turn around and aid those who would kill for us and for our ideas? Did God and Jesus say that the "godless peoples" should be converted or wiped out?

It's truly uncivilized and un-Christian to kill in the name of democracy, or any ideology for that matter. So why do we do it? I don't know. But I do know what it does to those we ask to do the killing and dying. It hurts our souls, or destroys them altogether. It hurts our hearts from generation to generation. My dad is an alcoholic for a lot of reasons besides the fact that he is a man of color who is also a war veteran. But still, the same experience has marked him and others like him forever.

Those kinds of trauma have a way of changing people's lives that they themselves may never sort out. But they go on just the same.

Yeah, Mr. or Mrs. American, I have a personal problem all right, but it's *your* problem, too! You probably are the same ones who beat the drums for more sacrificial lambs to go off and kill and die in the name of freedom and Christianity.

Whether I ever fully adjust and reintegrate myself into mainstream society is of less concern now. Because the way the process has settled with me now is that I feel there is no way in hell that I'm ever going to "feel good" about that experience. In fact, I believe the pursuit of this kind of settlement to be perverse and unhealthy to me as well as to my nation.

It used to hurt me when people would suggest that I simply had a personal vendetta to fulfill, or that I was a crybaby or that it would be better for me if I could just simply forget it. Right, just forget about it. Stuff it away and pour alcohol over it, as my dad does. But please, whatever you do, don't remind the rest of us about it! We don't want to hear it.

This has been my chance to tell anyone who cares, and even those who don't, that in some ways I'm better for the experience. But I'm also still bitter, and I will be as long as my country kills people on my behalf under the false premise of freedom for the same people we are killing. It just doesn't make any sense.

I refuse to romanticize my involvement or my country's in that horrendous war so that my country can "feel good" again. I refuse to accept ideological differences as justification of war.

I refuse to remain silent as long as we insist on pursuing military solutions to our differences with the communist world or the Third World. We are a warlike people, but we claim we are not. We have the capability to destroy the world, and we probably will do it!

I'm not crazy, and neither are those like me. For those who are quick to point a finger at us and say, "Oh, he's a Vietnam veteran, you know. You know about *them*. They're a little *off*, you know," I say this, "Don't bet on it!" I'm on my soapbox, but I'm far from crazy. What I have to say, and I'll say it until the day I die, is that we were wrong, and it is wrong to kill other people in the name of religion and ideologies. And no movie or parade, memorial or book, is going to make me "feel good" about the Vietnam War just so that my country can send others like me to kill on my behalf. I don't want you to die for me and my freedom, young man or young woman. Don't be fooled by all the flag-waving and drumbeating. That's not what it's all about. What war really is, is pain and suffering and then more pain and suffering. It never ends, no matter who wins. You lose, no matter the outcome. Even if you survive, it will be in your heart and soul for the rest of your life. So be sure it's worth that! Be sure you are answering a real and just threat and not just answering the call of a bunch of cold war warriors from the age of communist hysteria.

I'm pleased with myself now because I feel I can contribute something to future generations in this way. I hope that some good comes out of it, but I know it is difficult undoing this warlike identity we have.

Now, eleven years later, when I look at the conclusion I wrote in 1986, I realize I was still bitter. And while I haven't lost the convictions I had, some of the passion has dissipated, and I'm more at peace with myself. Writing about my family, and about my whole life, made me see the Vietnam War as just one part of my life. Perhaps it is and always will be the most important part or at least the most intense part, but I am at peace with it. I believe now that I'm better off for the experience because it forced me to be conscious about my life. Working on this book was a necessary spiritual journey; it wasn't just rehashing my life, it was coming to terms with my life.

I, and many other veterans like me, have made more progress than the country in dealing with the war. The country is still ill and neurotic about that war. As a Vietnam veteran, I feel that what I can contribute, and hope to continue to contribute, is to help heal the country, not just for my own sake but for all the lives that were sacrificed — Vietnamese and American. Teaching about it in whatever ways I can is something I will always be willing to do, and something I have an obligation to do.

I am determined to have a full life for the sake of those boys who were killed in the war, who would have liked to have had my life because it was a life. What I choose to take from the hell of Vietnam is a spiritual, productive, loving existence. And that's why I believe I'm healed, as much as I can be, for now. Time will take it from here.

Epilogue

I first decided to tell my story in 1986 in order to present the experiences of one Mexican-American in the Vietnam War. I felt it was important that we Chicanos not be forgotten, that we be recognized for our sacrifices and contributions, particularly because Chicano and other Latino soldiers suffered the highest casualty rates per capita of any group. Why? Because we were given the most dangerous jobs. As a result, we also suffered higher rates of post-traumatic stress syndrome.

Over the years I have struggled with my identity as a Chicano or Mexican-American. I once believed I knew who and what I was, but writing this book has forced me to scrutinize my identity. Now I can see how mixed up I have been. I believe I have come to terms with who I am.

I am of Mexican descent. Denying that I was Mexican was part of my upbringing and therefore part of my confusion. But I do not believe my parents wanted me to deny my heritage as a whole. They were trying to counter Anglo America's negative perceptions about us, perceptions that we were dirty, lazy, and dumb. My parents believed that speaking Spanish was a liability. It was a conscious decision on their part: We would not speak Spanish. They also believed it was detrimental to live in any semblance of a barrio. They truly believed it was important that we join the mainstream in every way — except in our hearts. For me this was a paradox with enormous implications. In the sixties, the advent of open cultural pride only seemed to confuse me more.

My attempts to reclaim or openly embrace my cultural heritage seem awkward now. I spent a lot of energy running away from the perception that I was a "coconut," a term used disparagingly in the Mexican-American and Chicano communities for someone who is "brown" on the outside and "white" on the inside. I felt shunned by the Chicano community because I was a coconut. But I wasn't accepted by mainstream society because I wasn't white. Recently racism among Chicanos against Mexican nationals, especially in California, has complicated matters even more for me. I have found myself resenting recent immigrants who are trying to make their way to a better life, just as my family did.

As I stated before, I am undeniably of Mexican descent. I am also without a doubt American, even as much as I am denied that designation by mainstream America. I am also, by some definitions, Chicano. Those who pride themselves in the Chicano designation sometimes deny me the same. I now can truly say, with much relief, that I am none of the above, yet I am a composite of all of the above. I am a composite of many characteristics, not unlike California, the place I have lived all my life.

In this book I don't speak for all Vietnam War veterans, all Chicano veterans, all Americans, or all Californians. The war was as complicated as it was long. My story is but one of millions. My hope is that we can use experiences like mine to think about issues beyond Vietnam veterans — the pain of the Vietnamese people or our country's propensity to police the world, for example. I also believe it is imperative that we get beyond damaging myths about the Vietnam veteran. Most of us have gone on with the business of living just like everyone else. There is no need to fear or pity us.

As for myself, I am resigned to the fact that I always will be perceived first as a Mexican immigrant. Regardless of how you see me, I am an American. Whether you call me that or not makes no difference. It can't be taken away. I am a patriot after all.